John Ogilvie

Philosophical and critical Observations

on the Nature, Characters, and various Species of Composition - Vol. II

John Ogilvie

Philosophical and critical Observations
on the Nature, Characters, and various Species of Composition - Vol. II

ISBN/EAN: 9783337076061

Printed in Europe, USA, Canada, Australia, Japan

Cover: Foto ©ninafisch / pixelio.de

More available books at **www.hansebooks.com**

PHILOSOPHICAL and CRITICAL

OBSERVATIONS

ON THE

NATURE, CHARACTERS,

AND

VARIOUS SPECIES

OF

COMPOSITION.

By JOHN OGILVIE, D. D.

IN TWO VOLUMES.

VOL. II.

Η πως αν αλλως συιςη τοδὶ ΤΟ ΠΑΝ, ει μη ΡΥΘΜΩ τινι και ΤΑΞΕΙ διεκεκοσμητο. Και τα υφ' ημων κατασκευαζομενα οργανα ΜΕΤΡΩ ΠΑΝΤΑ γιγνονται. Ει δε ΠΑΝΤΑ αλλα, πολλω γε μαλλον Ο ΛΟΓΟΣ, ατε και ΠΕΡΙΕΚΤΙΚΟΣ ΑΠΑΝΤΩΝ ΩΝ.
ΛΟΝΓΙΝ. ΑΠΟΣΠΑΣ.

Of all the arts in which mankind excel,
Nature's chief master-piece is WRITING WELL.
BUCKINGHAM.

LONDON,
Printed for G. ROBINSON, in Paternoster-Row.
MDCCLXXIV.

CONTENTS.

BOOK II.

Of Composition as distinguished by particular Characters and Species.

SECTION I.
Of the style of Composition in general, its distinguishing properties and defects. p. 1

SECTION II.
Of simple Composition,   37

SECTION III.
Of perspicuous Composition.   83

SECTION IV.
Of elegant Composition.   122

SECTION V.
Of sublime Composition,   158

SECTION VI.
Of nervous Composition.   199

SECTION VII.
Of correct Composition.   275

ERRATA.

Page 24. laſt line of the note, *after* Vid. *add* Liv. Hiſt. paſſim. P. 26. l. 3. *after* fable *add* when. P. 36. laſt line, *add* up to be peruſed as a taſk. P. 113. l. 22. *dele* mad. P. 130. l. 2. *for* thruſts *read* throws. P. 167. l. 9. *for* criteria *read* criterion. P. 171. l. 21. *after* when *add* an. P. 186. l. 11. *for* particularly *read* particularity. P. 202. l. 11. *for* is *read* are. P. 223. l. 22. *for* illuſtrations *read* illuſtration. P. 238. l. 12. *for* ſeparately *read* ſeldom. P. 246. l. 6. of the note, *for* allows *read* allowed. P. 262. l. 19. *for* caſes *read* cauſes. P. 280. l. 5. *for* criteria *read* character. P. 286. l. 1. *for* tells *read* tell. P. 331. l. 7. *for* abjurations *read* adjurations.

PHILOSOPHICAL and CRITICAL

OBSERVATIONS

ON

COMPOSITION.

BOOK II.

Of Composition as distinguished by particular Characters and Species.

SECTION I.

Of the style of Composition in general, its distinguishing properties and defects.

FROM the observations we have made in a former part of this work on Composition, as indicating the intellectual character, and as giving exercise to the powers by which man is distinguished in all their variety of combination; from these we are naturally led to consider the external marks or signatures by which we estimate

estimate in the various branches of the art (at least in a great measure) the excellence or defect of the artist's execution. This presents to us a view of this subject more pleasing perhaps than we have hitherto taken; and suggests at the same time the answer to an important enquiry;—by what method we may distinguish *genuine* from *apparent* beauty in the performances that fall under our examination; that faults by being perceived may be avoided; and genuine, not seeming excellence, may become the object of imitation.

It ought to be observed in the present, as in many other instances, that the difficulty of making this distinction is encreased more perhaps by a habit of trusting to the judgment of those whom we have been accustomed to hold in estimation, than from any inability in a great number of readers to think justly for themselves on this subject. It happens frequently that those who are diffident of their own sentiments are misled in their judgment of things by confiding implicitly in the decision of others, who, with inferior merit

perhaps

Observations on Composition. 3

perhaps to themselves, have pretensions incomparably greater; and imposed upon by an illusion which reason would have dissipated, permit their opinions to be influenced by false prepossessions, in matters of indispensable importance.

Among the almost innumerable expedients by which the judgment of mankind may be marked from its native bias, to form false as well as inadequate estimates, one of the most powerful is that prepossession which the mind naturally and justly entertains in favour of a work distinguished by judicious sentiments, in whatever dress these may be exhibited to observation. In such cases the attainment of an end of primary consequence makes us overlook a circumstance that is deemed to be comparatively insignificant; and even a reader, whose good sense might (if unbiassed in its decision) show him the proper value of both objects, is taught to under-rate the one, because perhaps he very properly thinks that too high an estimation cannot be formed of the other.

This remark (we may observe by the bye) is one of those which discover the imperfection of the human mind in a very striking point of view, and it extends as much to the various transactions of life, as to matters that may be deemed of pure speculation. Thus a beautiful and a deformed figure, presented at the same time before the eye, will impress ideas upon the soundest understanding, which an examination of each of these separately will enable it afterwards to correct. The faults of the former will be found to have escaped observation only as obliterated by the more glaring deformities of the latter; as on the contrary, beauties will be found in this last when contemplated apart, which the lustre of its companion has screened effectually from superficial investigation. Reflection will convince us that we form estimates equally inadequate almost always when objects of contrary natures are set in immediate opposition. The advantages arising from any acquisition are never seen in so striking a light, as when contrasted

with

with the lofs or the want of this benefit. We are ready in fuch a cafe to include every enjoyment in the poffeffion of the one, and every mifery in the approach of the other; contrary to that dictate of fober reafon which would foon convince us that the lofs of fome acquirements is as neceffary at one time to prevent fatiety, as the poffeffion of thefe at another is to conftitute happinefs.—But let us return from this little digreffion.

To obftructions arifing from the motives here enumerated, we may moft probably afcribe the little improvement which the ftile of philofophical Compofition received for fome ages after the fall of the Roman Empire. Thofe who profeffed philofophy in thefe ages collected the maxims without imbibing the fpirit of the ancients; and having obtained the reputation of thinking judicioufly in confequence of a few metaphyfical diftinctions, the obfcurity of an embarraffed and inelegant diction, like the hieroglyphical learning of Ægypt, was deemed a proper veil to fcreen their tenets from the cognifance of the vulgar *. Their readers, impofed upon by the pretenfions of their teachers to fuperior knowledge and underftanding, received their inftructions as oracles emitted by wifdom; which, conveyed in any form of words whatever, were either admitted as truths irrefragably certain; or admired, when not underftood, as indications of profound fagacity. In this manner the jargon of the fchools not only paffed upon the lefs intelligent for found philofophy, but even the errors of certain writers came to be held in veneration; and obfcurity of expreffion, the capital fault of the ftyle of Compofition, to be regarded as the myfterious vehicle of truths derived from the deepeft difquifition †.

While

---

* Among thefe the difciples of a philofopher were bound to take an oath. Εν υποκρυφοις ταυτα εχειν, και τοις απαιδευτοις και αμυητοις μη μεταδιδοναι.

Seld. de Diis Syr.

† The bad confequences that arofe from the abfurd, trifling, and fcandalous doctrines of the fchoolmen in the 12th, 13th, 14th, and 15th centuries, are now fo well known that it would be improper here to trace

While it fared thus with the noblest of sciences, the arts, whose improvement contributes

---

trace these at any length. We shall therefore only observe, as a remark connected with the present subject, that the barbarous language in which these were cloathed contributed as much as any other circumstance to prevent genuine philosophy from being at the same time sooner and more universally propagated. Instead of classical purity and elegance, Hales, Aquinas, Bonaventure, Achillini, Albertus Magnus, and many others of the same class, studied only a language suited to their own barbarous and unintelligible distinctions. One of these in particular (Achillini) carried to so great a length this talent of perplexing every subject by distinctions, that his acuteness was compared to that of the devil. "Fu acutissimo argumentatore (says an Italian historian, of the writers of Bologna) onde ne circoli dove argumentava e non era conosciuto, passò in proverbio qu'ell aut Diabolus, aut Achillinus." Orlan. Notiz. degli Scritt. Bologn Perhaps one reason which contributed principally to keep mankind for so many ages in ignorance of every thing but this jargon, which reason has now so totally exploded, was the state of modern languages then in their infancy, and unfit (from the multifarious dialects then blended together, but having formed no permanent standard) to convey the principles of any art or science whatever. Metaphysical subtleties, therefore, screened from censure by the sacred name of *Aristotelian philosophy*, were cloathed in a language refined by the efforts of a Tully and a Virgil; but these having been exploded by the Quodlibetarians, Sententiarians,

tributes to that of philosophy, with which these maintain a constant and indissoluble union,

---

Nominals, and Scotists*, (these *Vandals* of *science* who made havock of the *Roman learning* as much as their predecessors had done of its *empire*) the admiration of the vulgar was kept up not only by the apprehended importance of certain tenets, but by the very circumstance perhaps of their being unintelligible; and as the Roman language was studied only for the sake of a few hackneyed phrases, known likewise to a very small number, no man had either inclination or ability to expose the absurdity of their systems. The human mind however must have emerged in the course of so many ages from this state of Gothic ignorance, had not men's eyes been artfully dazzled by the splendor of an illustrious name, and one of the greatest benefactors of mankind rendered, by a strange perversion, the patron of absurdity and nonsense. It must, no doubt, be acknowledged, that some very abstruse distinctions in the logic and physics of Aristotle perhaps originally led the way to those verbal controversies, and unintelligible ænigmas, which were sanctioned by his authority. But nothing serves to discover more clearly the danger arising from an indulgence of this metaphysical subtlety than the consequences of which it became productive. The dreams which every distempered zealot conceived with regard to election, free will, predestination, &c. were retailed as the

---

* Of these parties some took their name from performances of Thomas Aquinas, entitled, Quodlibetical Propositions, Commentaries on the Sentences of Aristotle, &c. or from his name Thomas, or from that of Duns Scotus, the founder of another tribe.

union, were equally neglected; and genius, like a tree capable of bearing the richest productions, but rising uncultivated in a wilderness, displayed extravagant though luxuriant shoots, instead of that mature and beautiful assemblage which is the offspring of culture, industry, and attention *.

During

---

tenets of this great philosopher *; and the play of words introduced into philosophy, was screened from censure under the name of criteria, in imitation of the same model by whose aid the boundaries of truth and falshood may be always discriminated. " Di cio ce doveva in gran parte obligazione ad Aristotele, il quali se non si fosse adoperato in *distinguer operatamente i generi delli ragioni, noi mancavamo di molti articoli di Fede.*" Palavicin. Thus Composition in every sense of the word, was obliterated during the reign of these profound metaphysicians; and perspicuity of expression once lost, a man's learning and sagacity came to be estimated by assertions which could not be refuted by the human understanding, because they exceeded its comprehension.

* That imagination which is the principal characteristic of genius, differs in this important respect

* See the works of Thomas Anglus, who wrote in the 14th century. Others discovered in the works of Aristotle, the mysteries of the trinity and incarnation. At the same time these men were themselves so ignorant of the language in which Aristotle wrote, that one of them in a commentary on his works, mistaking the word αυλος for αυλης, a musical instrument, adduced thirteen propositions to prove that the soul of man is a pipe.

from

During the declension of the Roman empire, the arts which had flourished in the time of its maturity, decayed gradually as its

---

from the faculty of understanding with regard to the objects about which it is employed, that though the latter may, as we have seen, be perverted in its use to support trifling or even absurd propositions, and to render falshood plausible by subtlety of distinction; yet the genuine offspring of the former however uncultivated are always beautiful, and though in a savage or barbarous age, its range may be contracted within a narrower compass, or its procedure marked by excentricity and wildness, yet still there is something. even in this irregularity which the mind contemplates with delight, and approves by a natural and irresistible impulse. Of the truth of this observation we have a striking evidence presented to us by the present subject, as at the very time when philosophy was reduced by the schoolmen to the despicable situation above-mentioned, poetry cultivated by a great and original genius, produced fruit which every succeeding age has beheld with admiration. The learned reader will perceive immediately, that the person here referred to is the great Italian poet *Dante*, who flourished about the end of the thirteenth century; and was contemporary with the writers mentioned in the preceding note. Stimulated at the same time by the propensity of his genius, and by the most implacable resentment of his country's ingratitude, he produced a poem in that age of superstition full of the keenest and most pointed invective; in which, though deficient in disposition and in

its dominion became contracted, and its inhabitants, inſtead of cultivating theſe, which in claſſical purity of language *, he laviſhed the beauties of poetry in ſuch a manner on his ſubject, that, even two centuries after his death, Francis I. felt the ſting of that ſatire ſo forcibly which was levelled at one of his predeceſſors †, that unable to bear the ſarcaſm, he commanded it to be ſtruck out from the edition of his works then extant in France.—At a time when the world was ſtill buried in ignorance, the celebrated Petrarch ſucceeded to this original; and with a genius leſs daring and animated, but gentler and more amiable than that of the former, contributed to prevent a taſte for letters from being wholly extirpated, and to carry on the work of reformation. Theſe and ſome other writers formed a kind of barrier againſt the encroachments of the ſchoolmen; and by poliſhing gradually the language of their country, opened a way to that clear and comprehenſive philoſophy which ſucceeded to metaphyſical impoſture. The laſt mentioned poet in particular, wrote many pieces in the language of ancient Rome, which (as he was publicly honoured with the laurel) had their weight in rendering it more univerſally ſtudied. Claſſical elegance in this manner came gradually to be admired and imitated; and thoſe unintelligible quibbles which had been deemed the efforts of profound ſagacity, gave way to reſearches in which human na-

* This deficiency can only be imputed to the age in which he wrote. See Lillius Gerald. Hiſt. Poet.
† Charles of Valois, whoſe predeceſſor Hugh Caper, he ſtigmatizeth as the ſon of a butcher.

which are the offspring of tranquillity and opulence, were employed in repelling the assaults of northern barbarians, who, after many attempts, at last accomplished their destruction *. In these ages the spirit of a

---

ture was developed, and the *heart of man*, not the quodlibetical propositions, became the subject of philosophical enquiry. These poets however (and even Ariosto himself who lived in an age somewhat more enlightened) though we may contemplate them as lights hung out to illuminate some places amidst the general darkness that overspread other regions ; yet while they reformed mankind, participated themselves of the faults ascribed so justly to the ages in which they lived. In works of length a judicious reader will observe a striking defect of correct disposition universally taking place, which is one of the surest marks either of a mind inadequate to its subject, or of licentious freedom derived from the manners of an uncultivated and barbarous age. But with all these disadvantages the language in which these authors wrote was gradually polished by their efforts ; and as soon as men were led to examine the standards of Greek and Roman genius, which had fallen so long into disuse, the faults of Composition in these days of ignorance were detected and rectified, at the same time that a more improved age expelled their models of architecture, statuary, and painting.

* See the deplorable state of the empire at this time described by Ammianus Marcellinus, and St. Jerom, who prophetically foretell the fall of the Roman world.

nation

nation was depreffed while its acquifitions were gradually fubverted; and attention diverted from the cultivation of the beautiful, into the channel of the neceffary and more immediately important, was wholly engroffed by external tranfactions, or by fuperftitious terrors arifing ultimately from difappointment.

It is a remark which will be found univerfally characteriftical of mankind, that when the mind is damped and crufhed as it were, by a feries of unexpected and difpiriting incidents, it is apt to follow the lead of fuperftition, and to trace confequences to caufes wholly fictitious and imaginary when it cannot develope their real original. In Rome when in all its glory with regard to grandeur and conqueft, a dictator was formally elected to expel the peftilence by driving a nail into the wall of a temple*; and one of the greateft men whom Athens ever produced, was facrificed to the cabal of a few factious citizens

---

* Examples of this need not be adduced. They occur often in the hiftory of the Commonwealth while in its infancy.

artfully

artfully working on the superstition of the populace *. These, however, as both nations were still in their maturity, were only short eruptions of a flame which was smothered though not extinguished by the sudden extinction of the causes which gave rise to it. But during the decay of the immense empire of Rome as these causes operated more steadily and universally, their consequences are set in a very strong light, and lie immediately open to dispassionate enquiry. The minds of men were at this time occupied in every province of the empire by attending either to the ravages of the barbarous nations attacking it on all sides, or to the more alarming internal dissensions which divided the christian church, and gave full scope to the suggestions of superstition, as the growth of heterodox opinions, and not the general corruption of manners was deemed to be

---

* The incident here referred to, relates, as the learned reader will perceive, to Alcibiades, who was driven from his country to gratify the most absurd superstition, and with whom fell the glory and dominion of Athens.

the

the cause of every repeated disaster*.
Each sect had here a field to retort the
accusation from one to another; and while
men's hearts were heated with rancour and
animosity, or their dread excited by the
imminent danger of losing their possessions,
it is surely not to be wondered at, that their
sentiments became perplexed, their learning contracted, and their language inelegant.

' In this series of events it is that we are
to search for the true cause of the decline
of the finer arts, and of the darkness in
which for many ages these continued to
be inveloped. History affords us many

---

* The author here means only to take notice of those schisms in the Christian church which from their absurdity and inconsistence could not produce bad consequences of any kind, though the zeal of some good men who employed their pens to expose principles which would have been forgot in a few years had no notice been taken of them, contributed at the same time to sharpen the spirits of men against each other, and to render the contagion more universal. Thus it happened, that what would have been only contemptible became noxious; and men were raised into significance by misapplication of the means applied to render them the objects of ridicule or detestation.

examples

examples of barbarous nations who, after having fubdued people more improved than themfelves, have in the courfe of a few ages adopted the laws, the manners, and the learning of the conquered. Here however the cafe was altogether different. The fubdued nations became affimilated (at leaft in a great meafure) to their barbarous conquerors. Whence arifeth this ftriking difference?—From this caufe undoubtedly, that every object worthy of imitation (with regard to the circumftances above-mentioned) had been cancelled among the conquered nations before they fubmitted to a foreign yoke. The wretched remains of their former excellence were ftill indeed to be met with:—but thefe, infufficient to improve a people altogether uncultivated, were mixed with abfurd and extravagant hypothefes; by which means a group of diffimilar, often difcordant objects was prefented to the mind, which it required the efforts of mankind not in one but in many ages to expel as the offspring of error, and to fubftitute proportion and fymmetry in its room. Superftition in thefe these times, untamed by the dictates of temperate philosophy, suggested imaginary evils which passed immediately for realities; and these dreams inculcated in language swelling into fustian, chiming into quibble, loaded with ornament, or pointed with unmeaning antithesis, made an impression upon minds unacquainted with any superior style of eloquence, adequate in every respect to the purposes which it was calculated to produce.

There is, it will be observed, this invariable affinity betwixt sentiment and the language in which it is conveyed, that though the diction may be smooth and mellifluous when the thoughts are wholly superficial, yet when these last are just and pertinent, forced ornaments and little conceits are seldom or never to be met with in the other. Sentiments judiciously applied, and distinctly comprehended, support themselves by their own intrinsic worth, and require only to be placed before the mind in simple, clear, and appropriated words. The same remark may be applied to illustrations. These (which in all works of length are indifpenfable) may be made to reprefent their objects in a very animated manner, when the words are forcible without being turgid, and the image ftrong though perfectly natural. When language on the contrary is obvioufly ftrained, and the words thrown out of their natural arrangement into irregular combinations, there is generally fome correfponding affectation in the thought which will marr the effect arifing ultimately from all.

During the continuance of thofe ages that elapfed from the decline of the Roman empire after the removal of the imperial feat, to the revival of letters in the fixteenth century, the faults that we have thus enumerated as characterifing the ftyle of Compofition, we may affirm to have been principal caufes, not only of the ignorance and confequently the rude manners of men, but of the duration of both to fo diftant a period.—But in order to comprehend the truth of this affertion, it will be neceffary that we enter more clofely into the fubject.

In

In what light foever we confider mankind, very little reflection will ferve to convince us that the *drefs* in which objects are prefented to the mind is a circumftance demanding the greateft degree of attention. It is in this cafe with the intellectual powers as in common inftances with the external organ of perception. " As an
" object, perhaps naturally uninviting if
" not difagreeable, is rendered attractive
" by an happy choice and difpofition of
" ornament in the laft inftance, fo in the
" other, even trite fentiments and mode-
" rate elocution become ftriking and ani-
" mated when thefe are recommended by
" the mufic of harmonious expreffion *."
When deprived, on the other hand of this recommendation, the moft judicious thoughts lofe to every reader a great part of their energy, and appear at beft like Ulyffes in the rags of a beggar, difguifed, ungraceful, and difqualified to attract that attention which thefe might otherwife have

---

* " Nam quædam & fententiis parva, & elocutione modica *virtus hæc fola* commendat." Quintil. lib. ix. c. 4.

irrefiftibly arrefted. The ftyle therefore
of Compofition will claim from thefe con-
fiderations a very high degree of merit,
as upon this fingle circumftance depends
the impreffion which fentiments make
upon the mind *. It is true indeed, that
when in confequence of a great difproportion betwixt the intellectual faculties,
thoughts altogether fuperficial are fpun
out and elaborately decorated with fuper-
fluous drapery; a judicious reader will
foon be difgufted with fo obvious an in-
congruity, and the writer will accomplifh
no other purpofe than that of difcovering
the levity of an exuberant imagination
uncontrouled by the underftanding. But
even here we may obferve in a ftrong
light the effect arifing from mufical dic-

---

* Ουκ εομεθα δ'αρα την συνθεσιν αρμονιαν τινα εσαν λογων ανθρωποις εμφυτων, και της ψυχης αυτης, εχι της ακοης μονης εφαπτομενων ποικιλας κινεσαν ιδεας ενοματων, νοησεων, πραγματων, καλλες ευμελειας, παντων ημιν ευτροφων και συγγενων και αμα τη μιξει και πολυμορφια των εχυτης φθογγων το παρεςος τω λεγοντι παθος εις τας ψυχας παρεισαγεσαν. Λογγιν. περι Υψ. τμημ. λθ.

tion,

tion, as the ear is not only filled with the period, but the paſſions themſelves are often powerfully excited when reaſon receives but little information. It is reflection that detects the fallacy, by enabling us to diſtinguiſh the tinſel of pucrile fancy from the accurate and coherent inveſtigation of reaſon.

As it is thus obvious that the effect which any diſcourſe produceth depends in a great meaſure upon the propriety of well adapted expreſſion, it will follow that the ultimate ends of Compoſition cannot in any caſe be obtained when this propriety is neglected, and when ſomething unſuitable is perceived to take place betwixt the *things* inculcated in any branch of the art, and the language in which theſe are preſented to the mind. That the civilization of mankind was originally promoted by perſons who excelled in the higheſt ſpecies of this comprehenſive art; that during its maturity, nations the moſt admired flouriſhed in every circumſtance either agreeable or beneficial; that upon its decline the manners of men returned gradually back

back to their primitive rufticity; and that in all ages, without exception, it has been the principal vehicle of light, of knowledge, and of happinefs, as connected with cultivated life;—thefe truths in a following fection of this work it will be our bufinefs more particularly to enforce and illuftrate *. At prefent it is only proper to obferve, that in proportion as we admit all or any of thefe to be derived from this original, the language in which they are exhibited will appear to merit a greater or lefs degree of attention. That any means whatever may accomplifh the purpofe for which it is applied, we confider it always as expedient that this fhould not only be thoroughly comprehended, but that it fhould likewife be rendered agreeable. Neceffity indeed fometimes obliges us to turn our thoughts upon fchemes of utility, in the purfuit of which we enjoy only the fatisfaction of contemplating the end as making gradually its approach. But it will confift with every man's experience, that truths the moft important

---

* Book iv. fect. 1.

when

when conveyed in dry language, and far more when wrapt in obscurity, are commonly studied and understood by few from whose memory likewise these may easily be erased; and no purpose of general emolument can be effectuated while the path that leads to it is intricate and unfrequented.

In order therefore to extend the observation, to cultivate the minds, and to polish the manners of mankind, their first teachers considered it as principally requisite to clothe their instructions in the most captivating dress. Hence fable and allegory became the vehicles of moral sentiment in the first dawning of society*; and as this method of communicating it was conformable to nature, whose standard is unalterable, it continued to be pursued successfully when civilization had made much greater progress †. In many cases

---

* In the writings of Orpheus, Amphion, Linus, &c. not to mention the two perfect standards of the epopœa, the Iliad, and Odyssey.

† Such are the beautiful pictures of Prodicus and Cebes in particular, besides the many sublime allegories in the philosophy of Plato.

as that of the legiflator in particular) when this medium of knowledge could not be made ufe of, precepts, rules of conduct, and even treaties of war and peace betwixt nations, were expreffed with the utmoft perfpicuity and brevity, that thofe truths might be rendered univerfally intelligible whofe immediate end is the benefit of fociety, and in the expreffion of which exterior ornament would be wholly improper *. By thefe means the mafters of Compofition alternately edified and entertained mankind. The manners of men became infenfibly foftened, and the love of virtue was inftilled into the heart while their attention was arrefted by harmonious expreffion, or their judgment convinced

---

* The reader who would fee this truth evinced may have recourfe to many parts of the Greek or Roman hiftory, in both of which he will find the treaties made with different nations, particularly with the Greeks and Perfians, and betwixt the Romans and Carthaginians in the Punic wars, conceived in fuch fimple terms, and fo concifely expreffed as will fhow that perfpicuity beyond all other circumftances was ftudied by both nations in the relation of their mutual agreements; and that thefe may be exhibited as models of ancient accuracy and propriety. Vid.

by

by sentiments clearly as well as justly laid before them; those principles by whose aid the human mind is most powerfully impressed, were judiciously applied to for this purpose; and that design was accomplished to which means were so happily adapted in consequence of that knowledge which the first philosophers discovered of the nature of man.

In the whole process here carried on, it will be easy to discern the use, or rather the necessity there was for adorning science, when thus eminently useful, with the insinuating eloquence of modulating language*. Precepts of any kind are undoubtedly of advantage only as these are universally examined and understood. In order to be rendered thus extensively beneficial, it is requisite that these should be rendered intelligible to all, and so enter-

---

* " Et tamen omnium longitudinum & brevitatum in sonis sicut acutarum graviumque vocum (says the illustrious Roman orator) judicium ipsa natura in auribus nostris collocavit; aures enim vel animus aurium nuncio naturalem quandam in se continet vocum omnium mensionem, &c. See likewise Διονσ. Αλικαρνασ. περι Ξυνθεσ. Ονοματ. p. 30.

taining at the fame time by being inculcated as the morals of fome beautiful fable, this vehicle can be employed as to evince that their authors well underftood this important truth, that he alone poffeffeth true difcernment—" Qui mifcuit utile dulci,—who blends the agreeable with the inftructive."

Here it may perhaps be objected to our remarks on Compofition in general, and particularly to the importance of attending to expreffion, that in whatever language we clothe our fentiments thefe cannot be of fuch extenfive emolument as has been reprefented, becaufe the far greater number of mankind have in all ages fhown little tafte for the arts, and have neither inclination to ftudy, nor capacity to be improved by the beauties, however exquifite, which are here pointed out. But we may reply to this, that in order to be benefited by the art of which we treat, it was not neceffary that every man fhould have judged from perfonal experience of its utility, any more than it is that to be convinced that there are fuch cities as Paris and

and Rome, we must receive occular evidence by surveying these on the spot. Of the last we receive sufficient proof from testimony wholly unquestioned, and the first becomes subservient to all the ends we have mentioned, by refining the sentiments and manners even of a few whose natural abilities thus improved qualify them to render these advantages at last universal by their influence, example, and conversation. Philosophy, considered with regard to effects on practice, is often sufficiently understood by men who have never entered deeply into metaphysical speculation, in the same manner as the performance of an able musician will communicate the most delightful sensations to a man who neither understands the rules of music himself, nor is able properly to employ an instrument. In both cases it is only indispensably requisite that there should be masters excellent in their professions, and qualified from this excellence to bring emolument, or procure an high degree of pleasure to those with whom they are connected in society.

society. It will not be affirmed by any man that the Athenian people, though acknowledged to have been the most ingenious and polished of any upon earth *, were all of them orators of the first class, or were fitted to excel in any other species of Composition. A distinguished genius in philosophy, poetry, or eloquence, made his appearance among them at some times; and by exciting the curiosity, or interesting powerfully the passions of human nature in his cause, became a benefactor to mankind in general, though the persons more immediately benefited were disqualified to comprehend every part of his writings, and far more to imitate his example. In some ages, masters in almost all the departments of literature arose at once, like new constellations illuminating the horizon, and spread light all around them as they

---

* Cicero's panegyric on this people shows what they continued to be even in his time. " Eruditissimos homines Asiaticos *quivis* Athenienfis indoctus, non verbis, fed fono vocis, nec tam bene, quam fuaviter loquendo facile superabit." De Orat. lib. iii.

proceeded in their course *. By these means, however, the people of Athens became such judges of language, and so accustomed to the most delicate propriety of expression, that an old woman of this city is said to have known the celebrated Theophrastus to be a foreigner, notwithstanding a residence of many years at Athens, by the wrong pronunciation of a single word.

As states therefore and kingdoms were gradually civilized, as men of genius and letters brought Composition nearer to a

---

* The age of Pericles affords an example of the first mentioned improvement, as that great man carried eloquence to a pitch never before known in Athens, and may be said to have afforded a model not only to the orators of his own age, but to his successor Demosthenes, who carried the art to perfection. This was completed in the age of Socrates (as it may well be called) when that illustrious name, with those of Aristotle and Plato, dignified philosophy; in history appeared a Thucydides and Xenophon; in poetry an Æschylus, Euripides, Aristophanes, Sophocles, Menander; in eloquence Demosthenes shone with unrivalled lustre; while Apelles, Phidias, and Praxiteles, completed this illustrious catalogue by their distinguished eminence in painting.

state

state of perfection*; so as the art degenerated from this standard we shall find a cor-

---

* It is necessary here that we keep constantly in our eye one distinction betwixt the effects which the possession of immense wealth produceth usually upon the manners of a people, and those which attend the progress of literary pursuits. Experience hath evinced in all ages, that the most hardy nations are in the course of a few generations effeminated by opulence, and that every refinement of luxury will in time be substituted in place of frugal meals, athletic exercises, vulgar attire, and mean accommodations. The ancient Persians appear to have had all the advantages derived from this source in the greatest profusion, and the arts attendant on luxury seem likewise to have been in some measure cultivated. Science however, and art in its utmost perfection excludes effeminacy as much as rusticity from the manners of mankind, and preserving the medium betwixt these extremes, confers courage while it subdues ferocity, and gives an elegance of manners perfectly consistent with vigour and intrepidity. The Greeks, inspired by their philosophers and orators with the contempt of death, and with the love of their country, considered the *great king* with justice as a splendid barbarian, and surpassed his subjects as much in the atchievements of war as in the cultivation of the finer arts, by whose influence a nation is benefited and adorned. The Turks in the present age, and the Asiatic people in general, compared with these of Europe, exhibit an instance in all respects similar to the former. Enervated by luxury without having seized the means of preventing its consequences,

corresponding change wrought on the manners of men which at the same time indispensably lost their principal excellencies. Deprived of those schools in which the practice of virtue was powerfully recommended, while taste acquired elegance and exquisite sensibility, men relapsed into barbarity as they fell into ignorance; and that savage ferocity (dignified with the name of courage) and absurd ostentation (mistaken for grandeur) again characterized nations which the light of knowledge had enabled these to distinguish *. It is true, indeed, that the sciences

---

consequences, the inhabitants of the southern provinces are found by experience to want that spirit of enterprize which the desire of knowledge powerfully stimulates, and that unshaken fortitude in danger which ariseth from contemplating death as a secondary evil. On the other hand, we have lately seen a people in the northern regions of this continent barbarous in their manners, and exposed to the rigour of an inhospitable climate, polished gradually by the introduction of those arts which the others have neglected, and excelling in the qualities which we have now shown to be their inseparable attendants.

* In their jousts and tournaments particularly; in the sums that were lavished without taste when their princes

ences in appearance continued to be taught, and the arts were known perhaps by more than appellation: but both became at laſt only "magni nominis umbra." With regard to the former, had the purity of philoſophical *ſentiment* even remained in theſe ages of darkneſs, it could have produced no effect on manners when that of language had degenerated. But this ſuppoſition is not natural. Juſtneſs of ſentiment, and an happy perſpicuity of expreſſion, had the ſame period. As men were improved by philoſophy when rendered univerſally intelligible by ſimplicity of language, and attractive by appropriated decoration, ſo when theſe means of improvement ceaſed to exiſt, their effects were likewiſe at an end. In proportion too as the evil ſpread, no remedy having been applied in due time, the cure became ſtill a matter of more difficulty. It is in all caſes whatever much eaſier to deviate from the right path, than to recover it

---

princes met with each other, and in the numerous and barbarous retinues with which theſe affected always to be ſurrounded.

when

when we have wandered and fallen into a labyrinth.

———Facilis defcenfus Averni :—
Sed revocare gradum, fuperafque evadere ad auras,
Hoc opus, hic labor eft.——— V IRG.

When a few however began at laſt to obſerve the falſe lights by which they had been miſled, and to follow the true ones; beſides the almoſt infuperable difficulty of forming a juſt ſtandard themſelves, when error had every where become ſo prevalent;—the prejudices of men attached to certain modes, however irrational, were to be ſubdued; and that fatal obſtacle to all improvement among thoſe whoſe opinions are taken up at ſecond hand, a great name on their ſide of the queſtion, to be removed by a clear appeal to the deciſion of reaſon.

We have entered into this detail particularly on the preſent occaſion, as it enables us to aſſign its due value to an important branch of our ſubject, and may be of uſe to thoſe who having fixed their attention (where it no doubt ought principally to be fixed) on the arrangement and ſentiment of their work, have failed after

after all to render it of general utility by neglecting to cultivate the elegant and agreeable *. These men are chargeable with

---

* The ancient critics agree universally in their sentiments of the high value of the style of Composition, and their other writers conform exactly (as we shall see afterwards) to the rules which these lay down. Aristotle tells us, that a writer in prose ought only to use a looser and less ornamented rythmus than the poet, so that his style will be a kind of *carmen solutum*, as Quintilian calls it. ΡΗΤΟΡ. βιϐ. Γ. τμημ. γ. & η. Longinus strongly expresseth his judgment on this subject, by saying φως γαρ τω οντι ιδιον του νου τα καλα ονοματα. Περι Υψ. τμημ. μ. Dionysius Halicarnasseus confirms likewise the preceding theory when he justly observes, Πολλοι γουν Ποιηται, και Συγγραφεις, Φιλοσοφοι, και Ρητορες λεξεις πανυ καλας και πρεπυσας τοις υποκειμενοις εκλεξαντες επιμελως αρμονιαν δε αυταις περιθεντες εικαιαν τινα και αμυσον υδεν χρησον απελαυσεν εκεινα τα ωουα. Ετεροι δε, ευκαταφροντα και ταπεινα λαϐουτες ονοματα, συνθεντες δε αυτα ηδεως και περιττως πολλην της αφροδιτην τω λογω περιεθηκαν. Περι ΣΥΝΘΕΣ. ΟΝΟΜ. p. ii. edit. Lipf. The Roman orator adopts the very words of Aristotle in his Discourse on Eloquence. " Perspicuum est igitur numeris adstrictam orationem esse debere; carere versibus." De Orat. sect. 56. Again, he calls the style of Composition in the same treatise " optimus & præstantissimus dicendi effector & Magister." It would be as endless to enumerate the opinions

with a fault of the fame kind with that of a man, who, though poffeffed of the higheft intellectual merit would juftly meet with neglect, if not with ridicule, by pretending to frequent the beft company in an unfafhionable, flovenly, or antiquated drefs *.

As

---

opinions of the ancients with regard to the excellence and ufe of words juftly ranged and properly felected, as to mention the diverfified rules which they have laid down for the attainment of this purpofe. From thofe which we have taken notice of here, it ought not to be concluded that thefe great men either compofed themfelves in what may be termed a poetical ftyle, or recommend this to others who write in profe upon any fubject. The ancients indeed, infufed in general into their writings a much larger portion of the idioms of poetry (as we fhall fee afterwards) than would now be thought confiftent with purity of expreffion. But they mean to prefcribe only an attention to harmony, as univerfally neceffary, which they appear to have confidered themfelves as an unifon to the human heart. Images likewife the moft picturefque, they permit us to ufe in any fpecies of Compofition whatever, as tending to render a fentiment clear that might have been perplexed, and an addrefs animated which would have been overlooked. The two provinces however they require to be preferved wholly diftinct.

* No reader will here fo far miftake the author's meaning as to fuppofe that he intends to reprefent ftyle

As we have thus endeavoured by observations drawn from human nature, and confirmed by the evidence of history, to show the important ends which may be accomplished by cultivating the style of Composition, it is necessary, in order to complete our view of this subject, that we consider next what is the best method to obtain excellence in a point of such utility, by examining separately the various *characters* by which different themes require expression to be distinguished, and by pointing out *that fault* into which we may fall while pursuing too eagerly the opposite beauty. The principal characters of

---

style as the dress of sentiment, as equal with regard to its effects with those that accompany elegance or sordid negligence, in the attire of the body. The illustration drawn from this last is indeed just, in as much as meanness in either will expose a man to neglect; and the faults are therefore of *the same kind*; but there is this striking difference betwixt these, that though intellectual merit may render a man in the last instance universally agreeable as a companion, when his peculiarity in point of dress is overlooked, yet in the other case, a work however valuable, in consequence of its defect in language is known only to a few, and among these is only taken.

the

the style of Composition, according to that branch of the art which may be studied, are simplicity, perspicuity, elegance, strength, grandeur or sublimity, propriety. The faults opposed or allied to these are meanness, obscurity, affected prettiness, weakness, bombast, inaccuracy. To each of the former therefore we shall appropriate a separate section. The latter will naturally fall under our consideration as standing in relation, or in opposition to the first. In order to render this part of the work as complete as possible, we shall in the last place consider what may be termed omissions or defects, rather than blemishes in this matter, that these by being exposed may be avoided or rectified.

SECTION II.
Of Simple Composition.

SIMPLICITY of expression is a phrase often used by men who have not affixed to it any determinate meaning. The greatest number of men who are influenced in this matter by the judgment of others, either give their opinion at second hand, or think that the simplest style consists of plain words put together without strength, variety, or ornament; an advantage which will be possessed in a greater or less degree, in proportion to a man's deficiency of genius. A very small share of reflection is however sufficient to convince us that an opinion of this kind must be wholly irrational, as it would deprive Composition of that just variety of language with which subjects altogether different ought necessarily to be treated. The same just discernment which makes a man select such exterior decoration as is at the same time suited to his circumstances, and advantageous to his appearance, will enable him to pronounce, if equally unbiassed, that nothing can be truly beautiful in Composition which wants that decent ornament that in all cases is necessary to constitute excellence. A theme of importance, in order to be properly managed, demands a dignity of expression corresponding to the nature of the sentiments; and

and vulgar epithets ought here to be avoided with the utmost care, as tending to deprefs thefe beneath their proper level *. When ftriking images, or illuftrations of any kind ought neceffarily to be introduced, fimplicity is only violated by the ufe of phrafes wholly unappropriated :—but thefe, however diverfified, while neither meanly creeping, nor affectedly pompous, are juft fuch as genius may perhaps have dictated to the author; and the good fenfe of his reader will im-

---

* " Et quod facit fyllabarum (fays Quintilian) idem verborum quoque inter fe copulatio, ut aliud alii junctum melius fonet.—Rebus atrocibus verba etiam ipfo auditu afpera magis conveniunt. Et honefta quidem turpibus potiora femper; nec fordidis unquam in oratione erudita eft locus. Quod enim alibi magnificum, tumidum alibi. Et quæ humilia circa res magnas, apta circa minores videntur." Lib. viii. c. 3. In the fame fpirit a critic, formerly quoted, obferves, φημι δε τον βουλομενον εργασασθαι λεξιν καλην εν τω συντιθεναι τας φωνας οσα καλλιλογιαν και μεγαλοπρεπειαν η σεμνοτητα περιειληφεν ονοματα εις τυτο συναγειν· Ειρηται δε τινα περι τουτων Θεοφραςω τω φιλοσοφω κοινοτερον εν τω περι λεξεως, &c. ΔΙΟΝΥΣ. ΑΛΙΚΑΡ. Περι ΣΥΝΘΕΣ. ΟΝΟΜ. p. 15.

mediately

mediately approve. What one of the moſt ſenſible writers of antiquity ſays of *things*, may ſurely be applied here with propriety to words.

Eſt *modus* in *lingua* ; ſunt certæ denique fines,
Quas ultra citraque nequit conſiſtere rectum. Hor.

1. The ſimple therefore in Compoſition may be conſidered as ſtanding in a double relation to *words*, and to thoſe *images* with which language is ornamented. The ſtyle of a performance is *ſimple* when expreſſions are happily choſen, properly placed, and ſo well adapted to the nature of the ſubject that the mind perceives in them neither abundance nor defect. By the former the *force* of a ſentiment is deſtroyed; by the latter its grace and its perſpicuity. That taſte for variety which is natural to the human mind, operates with equal power on every ſubject that attracts its attention. A thought ſtrikingly characteriſtical of the heart or mind, and calculated on that account to make a very forcible impreſſion on an intelligent reader, when it is ſpun out and placed elaborately

in

in every point of view, fatigues inſtead of affording us either inſtruction or entertainment:—its force is gradually enervated, and at laſt it eſcapes obſervation. This fault is often imputable to authors of unqueſtioned genius, and generally to thoſe who have received a large proportion of imagination. In eloquence particularly, an orator is apt in this manner to violate ſimplicity by attempting to enlarge and amplify every part of his ſubject.—" As (ſays the eloquent Chryſoſtom)
" we admire a phyſician when we obſerve
" him reſtoring to perfect health perſons
" who had laboured under diſeaſes that
" were judged to be incurable; ſo, my
" beloved friends, behold with admiration
" and aſtoniſhment the actions of our Sa-
" viour, who could not only expel at once
" diſeaſes, however inveterate, from the
" body, but could render thoſe *in a moment*
" worthy of the kingdom of heaven who
" had attained to the very ſummit of
" wickedneſs.—To-day (ſaid he to the
" thief on the croſs) thou ſhalt be with
" me

"me in paradise *." Without remarking here on the illustration, as not perfectly adequate to its object, I shall only observe, that the sense at these last words is complete, and the words of scripture are significant and striking. But when our celebrated orator lengthens out this description by talking of the μεγαλη τιμη, πολυ της φιλανθρωπιας το μεγεθος, αφατος η υπερβολη της αγαθοτητος, great dignity, immense philanthropy, and inexpressible overflowing of love discovered in this transaction, every reader will be ready to think that an animated stroke of eloquence is here enervated by an amplification inconsistent with simplicity.

As this character of the style of Composition appears thus to be incompatible

---

* Καθαπερ οιουν ιατρον τοτε θαυμαζομεν οταν ιδωμεν οτι ανθρωπους ανιατα νοσηματα εχοντας απαλλαξας της αρρωςιας προς καθαραν υγιειαν επανηγαγεν· ετω και του ΧΡΙΣΤΟΝ θαυμασον αγαπητε και εκπλαγηθι οτι λαβων ανιατα νοσηματα ψυχης εχοντας ανθρωπους ιχυσε και της κακιας απαλλαξαι, και της των ουρανων βασιλειας αξιους αποφηναι τους προς την εσχατην πονηριαν εληλακοτας. Σημερον μετ' εμου εση εν τω Παραδεισω. ΧΡΥΣΟΣΤ. εις το ςαυρ. p. 488.

with

with improper diffusion, so it is in other cases equally violated by the affectation of brevity. The mind, like the body, is equally debilitated by too much, and by too little exercise. It perceives immediately a defect of expression when the parts of a subject are not shown in their full proportions, and when thoughts are crouded so closely together that it requires the force of constant recollection to contemplate these apart. A noble and striking sentiment is often overlooked by an error of this kind, just as a single figure though intensely animated may escape the eye in a piece of history-painting, by being improperly placed in a promiscuous group. An object delineated with simplicity is one in which all is uniform, regular, and consistent. When these succeed one another with too much rapidity, regularity can no longer be attended to in their disposition; and instead of being presented to the mind in a *suitable* dress, such objects cannot be said with propriety to have any form whatever.

Should

Should it be said after all, that the affectation of concifeness which is cenfured here, is rather in general deftructive of *perfpicuity*, than inconfiftent with *fimplicity* of language, we may anfwer, that if the latter can only be obtained when an idea is expreffed in the fitteft words, and is exhibited in a drefs at the fame time unoftentatious and attractive, it will follow that when language wants thefe diftinguifhing qualities it can with no more propriety be denominated fimple, than this epithet would characterife the appearance of a man whofe clothes were difproportioned to the fhape or fize of his body; and deftitute of that beautiful fymmetry which gives eafe as well as dignity to the deportment.

Among the ancients there is perhaps no writer who more frequently lofeth fight of fimplicity by this affectation of peculiar brevity, than the fatyrift Perfius. Perhaps indeed of all the other branches of Compofition, fatire is that in which it is moft neceffary to render a ftroke energetical by a mode of expreffion at the fame time concife concise and forcible. But the poet above-mentioned will surely be deemed by every intelligent reader to have erred in attempting to imitate this beauty. The very first lines of his poem present to us sentiments that appear disjointed, because the language is defective in which these are represented.

O curas hominum! O quantum est in rebus
 inane!—
Quis leget hæc?—Min' tu istud ais?—Nemo her-
 cule Nemo.
Vel duo, vel nemo.—Turpe, & miserabile. Quare?
Ne mihi Polydamus, & Troiades Labeonem
Pretulerint.—Nugæ, &c.

In these verses the thoughts obviously seem to want connection, from too scanty a proportion of words. After having mentioned the vanity of human enjoyments, we are not aware that the expression " Quis leget hæc?" which is abrupt enough in the beginning of the second line of his satire, is designed to strike at the manners of the Romans, then so degenerated as to read nothing that bore the semblance of morality. Again, in the

lines

lines immediately following, the sense requires him to have said—" As Hector was "afraid left the Trojans should prefer "Polydamus to him, so am I alarmed lest "our Polydamus (Nero) should prefer "Labeo to me."—But by leaving out the word (vereor) "I am afraid" the sense is left uncompleted.—We might mention examples of the same fault in more modern writers than Persius*. But what has been already said we presume is sufficient to illustrate our view of this subject, and to dwell on the faults of an eminent author longer than such an illustration may require, is altogether disagreeable.

Let us observe, however, that the style of Composition, considered as a vehicle of thought which ought to be justly adapted to its object, is in the above-mentioned instance principally defective in that simple description which demands the whole to be plainly and consistently represented.

---

* In the Satires and Night Thoughts of Young, the reader will meet with instances of the fault here censured, arising most probably from that *rapidity of thought* (if we may thus express it) which often characteriseth the highest degree of genius.

When

When the language of any work is on the other hand judiciously adapted to the sentiments, the perusal of it affords the mind that perfect satisfaction which (though unknown to ourselves) is really the consequence of having obtained an accurate imitation of nature. In philosophy and history, as well as in such works as are more immediately addressed to the imagination, this correspondence of expression and thought hath the same uniform and unvaried effect. Every man is ready to think, that placed in similar circumstances he would have thought or spoke in the same manner as the author, because in fact he hath adopted the language not of an individual, but of human nature.

There is no mistake more common, and at the same time susceptible of easier refutation, than that which would confine simplicity to some particular species of Composition, when in reality it constitutes the principal ornament of all. Though pastoral poetry, obvious narration, or descriptions of still life are the usual spheres of this excellence, in which it ought invariably

riably to predominate, yet we shall find upon trial the sublime, the picturesque, the nervous, and the pathetic, to be distinguished when in their highest perfection by the being conveyed in words the most simple and artless. We shall here produce examples of each.

Of genuine sublimity, a stroke universally acknowledged to be one of the noblest that ever entered into the mind of man, is in the account given by Moses of the creation*. " Darkness (says he) was " upon the deep, and the spirit of God " moved upon the face of the waters.— " And God said—*Let there be light, and* " *there was light !"*—This example of divine eloquence, expressed in words so suited to the majesty of the speaker, agrees exactly with our description of *simple* Composition, as consisting of words happily selected, in which the mind perceives neither abundance nor defect.—In a similar spirit of sublime simplicity does Milton pourtray the shield of Satan, and the atti-

---

* Genes. i. 3.

tude of this prince of hell treading on the burning lake.

He scarce had ceased when the superior fiend
Was moving tow'rd the shore;—his pond'rous shield
Behind him cast,—the broad circumference
Hung on his shoulders like the moon!—Par. Lost, b. i.

Let the reader try whether this description (so completely exhibiting its object) would bear either the addition or transposition of a single word without being impaired. Yet here is no ornamental epithet. The words themselves and their arrangement are the most natural and simple that can be conceived.—Apollo in the Iliad leading on Hector to the destruction of Greece, and levelling the mound which the people of that nation had reared for their defence, affords us an example in all respects adequate to the former.

—— Προπαροιθε δε Φοιβος Απολλων
Ρει' οχθας καπετοιο βαθειης ποσσιν ερειπων
Ες μισσον κατεβαλλε· γεφυρωσεν δε κελευθον
Μακρην ηδ' ευρειαν.——
Τη ρ' οιγε προχεοντο φαλαγγηδον, προ δ' Απολλων
Αιγιδ' εχων εριτιμον, ερειπε δε τειχος Αχαιων
Ρεια μαλ'.—— ΙΛΙΑΔ. Ο:.

Apollo planted at the trench's bound
Push'd at the bank; down sunk th' enormous mound:

Roll'd in the ditch the heapy ruin lay,
A sudden road, a long, and ample way!——
The wondering crouds the downward level trod,
Before them flamed the shield, and march'd the God;
Then with his hand he shook the mighty wall,
And lo! the turrets nod! the bulwarks fall! &c. *

As in the examples above-mentioned we obferve the fimpleft words conveying the moft fublime ideas, fo in what follows thefe appear to conftitute *the moft picturefque* defcription. An example of this kind incomparably animated, occurs in the fourth chapter of Job, where Eliphaz relates his interview with an inhabitant of the invifible world, in fuch language as placeth every circumftance of this tranfaction before the very eye of the reader.—" In thoughts from the vifions of the night, when deep fleep falleth on men,—fear came upon me and trembling, which made all my bones to shake. Then a fpirit paffed before my face: the hair of my flefh ftood up. It ftood ftill, but I could

---

* We have here given Pope's tranflation, in which a reader of tafte may perhaps think, not unjuftly, that though the *fublimity* of the original is in this paffage improved, yet its *fimplicity* is in a great meafure loft.

not

not difcern the form thereof. An image was before mine eyes:—there was filence, and I heard a voice."—What fimplicity is here in the expreffion! yet what ftrength and vivacity in the colouring!—Without the aid of a metaphor, the infpired writer fets before our eyes a picture fo calculated to excite the moft exquifite feelings, that it was drawn (one fhould think) by the pencil of nature herfelf.

Virgil (though his excellence appears to lie rather in throwing pathetic than picturefque circumftances into his defcriptions) yet has wrought up a picture of the fame kind with that already mentioned, in his account of the ghoft of Hector, remarkable for the beauties pointed out in the former.

—— Ecce ante oculos mœftiffimus Hector
Vifus adeffe mihi, largofque effundere fletus!
.. Raptatus bigis ut quondam, aterque cruento
Pulvere perque pedes trajectus lora tumentes:
Hei mihi qualis erat!——   Æneid. lib. ii.

This mixture of the picturefque and pathetic, expreffed with the moft beautiful fimplicity, characterifeth the attitude of Priam in the Iliad, befeeching his fon to

enter the city and shun Achilles.
Ωμωξεν δ' ο γερων, κεφαλην δ'ογε κοψατο χερσιν
Υψος αναχομενος, μεγα δ'οιμωξας, εγεγωνει
Λισσομενος Φιλον υιον—

The simplicity as well as picturesque beauty of the original is well preserved in the translation.

    Then wept the sage
He strikes his reverend head now white with age;
He lifts his wither'd arms, obtests the skies;
And calls his much-loved son with feeble cries. POPE.

If in the instances above referred to, the sublime and picturesque in Composition appear to be consistent with perfect simplicity of language, nervous and forcible description is equally compatible with, and adorned by this distinguishing excellence. As a proof of this we find Xenophon, who among all the historians of antiquity excels in the beautiful simplicity here recommended, using words, when the occasion demands it, full of energy and significance. In the account of Cyrus's battle with Crœsus, we meet with some striking examples to this purpose. " There
" was then (says he, describing the heat
" of the battle) a desperate engagement
          " with

" with darts, lances, and swords, com-
" menced on both sides.—There was
" great slaughter of men, terrible clashing
" of arms, and a tumultuous clamour
" raised on all hands; some congratulat-
" ing their companions, some exhorting
" the fearful, and some imploring the
" Gods."—When Cyrus's horse a little
after is wounded, the consequences are
thus concisely, but energetically described.
" Then (says he) you might have seen
" of what advantage to a prince is the
" love of his subjects. For instantly all
" shouted at once, and rushed impetu-
" ously to the battle. They drive, and
" are driven; strike, and are struck. One
" of Cyrus's attendants in the mean time
" dismounted, and placed him on his own
" horse. But when on horseback, look-
" ing around him, he saw the Ægyptians
" slaughtered on all sides *." The historian

---

* The author hath translated this passage in the text, lest some readers should be frightened at the sight of so much Greek. But the original is too beautiful to be omitted, and incomparably beyond any translation.

Ἔνθα

torian was sensible that ornament of any kind in a detail of this nature would have been wholly unappropriated. He is therefore principally intent upon making the words correspond as justly as possible to the things represented by them. Superfluous epithets are therefore avoided; and there is a strength in the expressions which conveys to us an idea of that desperate perseverance with which the battle was carried on.—So consistent is the most perfect simplicity with that vigorous language which renders an idea distinct by its propriety of phrase, and its impression dur-

---

Ενθα δε δεινη μαχη ην και δορατων, και ξυςων, και μαχαιρων.—Ην δε πολυς μεν ανδρων φονος, πολυς δε κτυπος οπλων και βελων παντοδαπων; πολλη δε βοη των μεν ανακαλευτων αλληλης, των δε παρακαλευομενων, των δε θεους. επικαλημενων.—Ενθα εγνω αν τις οσον αξιον ειη τον φιλεισθαι αρχοντα υπο των αρχομενων. Ευθυς γαρ ανεβοησαν και τε παντες και προσπεσοντες εμαχοντο· εωθεν, εωθυντο, επαιον, επαιουτο. Καταπηδησας δε τις απο τε ιππε των τε Κυρε υπηρετων αναβαλλει αυτον επι του εαυτε ιππον. Ως δε ανεβη ο Κυρος κατειδε παντοθεν ηδε παιομενους τες Αιγυπτιους, &c. ΞΕΝΟΦΩΝΤ. Κυρ. Παιδ. βιβ. ζ.

able

able by an energy suited to the nature of the object.

Simple Composition, considered as consisting of well-adapted words without taking in adventitious ornament, thus characteristical as it is of the sublime, the picturesque, and the nervous in this art, yet in no case whatever is seen to higher advantage than when we assume the language, or paint the consequences of passion. We have observed in a former section of this work, that a mind agitated by the conflict of passions never adopts a metaphor to express its feelings. A sudden exclamation just inspired by the occasion, has an effect upon every mind at these times, superior to that which the most artful assemblage of mellifluous and ornamented periods could ever have produced. Art never indeed appears so disgusting as when we discover it (however affectedly concealed) in any purely pathetic representation. In an account of this kind indeed the passions may be gradually wrought up to the utmost height by a progressive and elaborate detail; but in such

such a process the author is required to conceal his address at the time; and though upon a closer scrutiny we may observe it with admiration, yet we justly impute a defect of judgment to him who lets us enter too suddenly into his design, as such a conduct always defeats the ultimate purpose of his work.

There are, we may observe, two methods of rouzing the passions to the most strenuous exertion, both of which, though different in other respects, yet agree in requiring simplicity of diction. One is when a climax is carried on, either in reasoning or in description, from lesser to more important objects, until the whole becomes highly and universally interesting:—the other ariseth from some judicious and happy imitation of nature in a particular occurrence, when her language is so significantly adopted as to make a powerful, as well as immediate impression upon the heart. The difference betwixt these lies principally in this, that the effect produced by the first method is slowly accomplished, though an entertainment agree-

agreeably protracted prepares us imperceptibly to feel it with energy; whereas the laſt preſents a picture whoſe force we immediately acknowledge, and which without preparation makes its way to the heart. Of the former kind are thoſe repreſentations which either ſet one event in a ſtrong and particular point of view, or derive their power from a detail of circumſtances. Here we permit the writer to expatiate at leiſure on every topic of perſuaſion, every ſentiment of compaſſion, every event in which we diſcover even a remote connection with the principal cataſtrophe. That a ſkilful artiſt may by theſe means irreſiſtibly ſtimulate the paſſions, as well as excite the affections of his audience, will not be diſputed by any perſon who is acquainted with either. Yet he who placed himſelf in circumſtances of diſtreſs, or happily imitating that of another, hits off an expreſſion which every mind appropriates as its own, poſſeſſeth this peculiar advantage that he takes the heart as it were by ſurprize; and to the paſſion, of whatever name, excited

cited by him fuperadds this feeling by which it acquires incomparable poignancy and power. In both cafes, (the laft however more particularly) we fhall find the fimpleft language producing the happieft effect. We fhall here adduce examples of each.

The celebrated ftory of Lucretia, as told by Livy, affords us a fignal example of the pathos with which a few unadorned expreffions may convey an interefting event to the mind. This heroine, after having fuffered an indignity which fhe determined not to furvive, fent one meffenger for her father, and another for her hufband.—" When thefe arrived (fays the
" hiftorian) they found Lucretia fitting
" difconfolate in her chamber. Her tears
" ftreamed at their entrance. To her
" hufband's queftion, whether all was well
" with her:—No, replied fhe; what can
" be well with a woman who has loft her
" honour?—The footfteps of another,
" O Collatinus, faid fhe, are in your bed.
" But my body alone is violated:—my
" mind is innocent. Let death be my
                              " wit-

" witnefs."—After having then concifely related the tranfaction, fhe adds in a fpirit of true heroifm.—" I, though guiltlefs of
" crime, exempt not myfelf from punifh-
" ment, nor fhall ever violated chaftity
" live by the example of Lucretia. She
" pierced her heart, when fhe had fpoke,
" with a knife concealed under her gar-
" ment, and falling forward in the pangs
" of death, expired *." In this pathetic tale, related with inimitable fimplicity, we are dazzled by no adventitious ornament;—a juft and beautiful affinity takes place betwixt the tranfaction and the words employed to defcribe it. The hiftorian paints the whole with a fpirit ade-

---

* " Lucretiam fedentem mœftam in cubiculo inveniunt. Adventu fuorum lacrymæ obortæ :—quærentique viro fatifne falva ? " Minime, inquit, quid enim falvi eft mulieri amiffa pudicitia! Veftigia viri alieni, Collatine, in lecto funt tuo : ceterum corpus eft tantum violatum, animus infons. Mors teftis erit."—
". Ego me ifti peccato abfolvo, fupplicio non libero. Nec ulla deinde impudicitia Lucretiæ exemplo vivet." Cultrum quem fub vefte abditum habebat, eum in corde defigit, prolapfaque in vulnus moribunda cecidit." Hiftor. Rom. Scriptores Omn. tom. i. p. 18. Aurel. Allob.

quate

quate to the greatness of the action. The crime was quickly committed; the resolution immediately taken, and unexpectedly executed. The language is therefore perfectly concise; and this correspondence betwixt the colour and the pattern imitated (if we may thus express it), this seemingly artless, and easy narration, conveys the whole with an energy, which elaborate description, if it had not annihilated, must have greatly impaired.

As we observe a pathos of the strongest kind to be excited in this instance by the narration of one event, in the following passage the same unaffected simplicity characterizeth the language when the detail is copious and circumstantial.—Tacitus, after having related the life of the celebrated Agricola, and expatiated on the cruelty of the tyrant whom he served, at last addresses his shade in a noble style of pathetic eloquence.—" Happy Agricola
" wast thou (says he), as thy life was illus-
" trious, and thy exit seasonable.!—From
" those who witnessed thy last scene we
" know that thy fate was supported with
                            " chear-

" chearfulnefs and refolution, as if thou
" wouldſt have configned thy innocence
" as a legacy to thy prince! But to me
" and thy daughter, befides the bitternefs
" of reflecting on a loſt parent, our grief
" is augmented, becaufe we had it not in
" our power to watch thee in ficknefs;
" to relieve the languor of declining na-
" ture; to fatiate our defires by gazing
" on, and embracing thee!—Beſt of pa-
" rents!—Every thing was then no doubt
" performed to thy honour by the moſt
" affectionate of conforts:—but fewer
" tears, in confequence of our abfence,
" were fhed at thine obfequies; and thy
" dying eyes expreſſed unfatisfied defire.
" If there is a place for the fpirits of the
" juſt;—if (as philofophy affures us) great
" minds furvive the ruin of the body;
" ferene be thy repofe*!"—In this ad-
dreſs

---

* " Tu vero felix Agricola non vitæ tantum cla-
ritate, fed etiam opportunitate mortis. Ut perhibent
qui interfuerant noviſſimis fermonibus tuis, conſtans
& libens fatum excepiſti, tanquam pro virili portione
innocentiam principi donares. Sed mihi filiæque
præter acerbitatem parentis erepti auget mœſtitiam
quod

dress the reader will observe a climax finely conducted throughout, the last words of which particularly have, from an abruptness perfectly natural, a very striking effect.

The impression made upon the heart in these, and in many other instances of a similar kind, after all becomes no doubt weaker in some degree, as during the whole process we observe the purpose which all is meant to effectuate. There is likewise an appearance of art in the round of modulated periods, however seemingly flowing and easy, which prevents an appeal, how forcible soever, from having irresistible energy.—But in that kind of pathos which is produced by a sudden exclamation, strongly expressive of internal feeling in any interesting occur-

---

quod assidere valitudini, fovere deficientem, satiari vultu complexu non contigit.—Omnia sine dubio, optime parentum, assidente amantissima uxore superfuere honori tuo:—paucioribus tamen lacrymis compositus es, & novissima in luce desideravere aliquid oculi tui. Si quis piorum manibus locus, si, ut sapientibus placet, non cum corpore extinguuntur magnæ animæ, placide quiescas!" Id. tom. ii. p. 279.

rence,

rence, the effect is at the fame time powerful and univerfal, becaufe the principles here wrought upon are common to all. Here we may foon be convinced that declamation or external ornament would be arguments of an exceedingly defective underftanding.—Nature, in circumftances of deep diftrefs, has one voice in every heart; to imitate which juftly is to excite the moft powerful principles of perfuafion that operate on mankind. In this cafe, a man may be faid to fpeak as if he had been deputed by the whole fpecies, every individual of which adopts his language as his own. The exclamations of David when he heard the account of Abfalom's death, are fuch as we may fuppofe that every father would make ufe of in fimilar circumftances. " O Abfalom, my fon! my " fon! Would to God that I had died for " thee! O! my fon, my fon Abfalom!"— There is inexpreffible pathos in thefe fhort repetitions, as they fhow a mind wholly engroffed by the contemplation of one object, and unable to depart from it for a moment.

When

When Creon, in the Antigone of Sophocles, finds that by having commanded the sister of Polynices to be buried alive, he had occasioned the death of his own wife and son, how perfectly natural is his behaviour!—" Alas! alas! (says he) why "does not some man plunge a hostile "weapon into my heart?—I, unhappy "wretch, was thy murderer*!"—Deaf to the consolation of his friends, his mind dwells only on one unhappy object.— " Ah! (says he) my son! my wife! I " killed you not willingly†!—Wretch

---

* Αι, αι, αι, αι,
Ανεπταν φοβω· τι μ' υκ ανταιαν
Επαισεν τις αμφιθηκτω ξιφει;
Αθλιος ιγω, &c.
Εγω γαρ σ'εγω κανον μελεος
Εγω φαμ' ετυμον.
† Αγοιτ' αν ματαιον, ανδρ' εκποδων
Ος ω παι σε γ' υχ εκων κατεκτα
Ος σε τ'αυταν. Ο μελεος, υδ' εχω
Οπα προς ποτερον ιδω·———
Ιτω, Ιτω
Φανητω μορων ο καλλις' εμων
Εμοι τερμιαν αγων ημεραν
Υπατος. Ιτω, Ιτω
Οπως μηκιτ' αμαρ' αλλ' εισιδω.
ΣΟΦΟΚ. Αντιγ.

" that

"that I am; where shall I fly?—Come,
"O death, to my relief, that I may never
"behold another day." In thefe examples it is not the poet, the orator, the man of fenfibility; it is the father and the hufband that fpeak. A fcene like this puts us in mind of an ancient portico, temple, or city, viewed in perfpective: Upon contemplating thefe for fome time we forget the art of the engraver, and ftand beneath the mouldering obelifks of Tadmor; walk through the portals of Perfepolis; recline in the apartments of Darius, and behold the great originals of ancient majefty and dominion.

II. Having thus confidered fimplicity of expreffion as adorning every branch of animated Compofition, when no foreign illuftrations are made ufe of, it remains, in order to complete our view of the prefent fubject, that when it becomes neceffary to introduce thefe, we enquire what it is that conftitutes fimplicity in the ornamental beauties of difcourfe.

As there is nothing which fets every part of a fubject in a more attractive light than

than just and apposite images, so the style of Composition requires not, in any point of view, greater delicacy and attention in order to receive the last heightening than in the present. It is, indeed, a matter of the greatest difficulty to cull out from the store of imagination, those natural ornaments which give colour and beauty to the arguments of reason; and to proportion these so exactly to the object, as at the same time to take in every part of it at once, and to render its impression forcible and permanent. All this is included in the idea of perfect simplicity. A series of argumentative sentiment, however powerfully it may for some time arrest attention by conveying new evidence to the understanding, yet in consequence of that uniform Composition, which must here be carried on, often becomes tedious, and when the thoughts are abstracted is almost unavoidably obscure, when it is not diversified with proper illustrations. These are like little openings in a country, otherwise uniformly cultivated, which at the same time that they present some new object to

the

the eye, beginning to be satiated with its former view, contribute to set off to the highest advantage such as are already familiar. There are few men in whose minds imagination is so defective, as not to suggest many of these ornaments in the conduct of an extensive work:—but the judgment of a writer appears in nothing more conspicuous than in their propriety and disposition. A sensible mind will be offended immediately with a group of illustrations, promiscuously scattered over a performance without much experience; because, even though these may be well appropriated to their objects, it is still at a loss to discover their use. Disgust ariseth as much from viewing too profuse, as too scanty a proportion of illustrations, because these, in fact, lose their name when applied to truths which are easily comprehended, and which require only to be perspicuously expressed. The simplicity of nature is here likewise violated, inconsistent as it is with the glare of ostentation.

In order to preserve this inimitable excellence in the ornaments of discourse, it is likewise necessary that the image should exhibit a complete representation of its original, by bringing every part of it successively into view. The principal design with which metaphors are introduced, is either to explain some truth which would have been obscure, or to render some sentiment striking which would have failed otherwise to excite observation. To accomplish the former of these ends, the object must be fully and distinctly represented to the mind by an image, as the face is shown in a mirror; and to obtain the latter, it must be placed judiciously in that point of view which contributes most effectually to display its propriety. That an object may be distinctly placed before the mind, it is requisite that the metaphor which conveys it should be followed out just as far as illustration requires, and no farther. Simplicity, as we have already evinced, excludes every degree of superfluity. When images are opened, expanded, and traced elaborately through a

variety

variety of circumstances, the mind loses sight of the original idea:—its proportion is no longer observed, and attention flags insensibly because it is not kept awake by the current of sentiment. We may observe likewise, that in philosophical, or even sentimental performances (as they are called), this attention to extend and expatiate upon every minute circumstance of an illustration, usually indicates sterility both of the reasoning and inventive faculty. Of the first, because thoughts in this case appear to rise very slowly when the mind is so intent upon drawing out each with every possible enlargement:— of the last, because a vigorous imagination is displayed by the variety, not the laboured decoration of its images; and by rendering each significant, but neither tedious nor overwrought.

While we avoid in this manner the error of pursuing images too closely, we must take care not to fall into the opposite extreme of *mixing* these improperly. This fault is occasioned by our taking only a partial view of an illustration by which its disproportion to the original in some particular circumstance escapes observation. In order to make the whole complete, the mind adopts insensibly some similar metaphor, and thus jumbles separate images together in the same description. A great genius is often led into this fault, by giving a loose to the exuberance of imagination. When Demosthenes, speaking of Æschines says, that after lying in wait to destroy an honest or upright member of the commonwealth, as soon as he has found an opportunity to accomplish his purpose, " he bursts like a tempest from his place of retreat;" the image here employed is no doubt incomparably expressive and significant.—But when immediately after he is described with the orator's other enemies, " like a wild beast furiously assaulting him;" and in order to preserve the force of both illustrations he concludes with saying, that such assaults had failed of " rendering him *cold* in the cause of his country," we are sensible of an improper mixture of images. An adversary sallying out like a whirlwind, and carrying

carrying all before him, may be compared with propriety to a tempest freezing and desolating the earth. But the beauty of the first epithet (chilling or freezing) is lost when considered as a consequence arising from the assault of a wild beast, and the images are therefore said to be blended improperly. The reader will find many examples of this fault, even in the best works both ancient and modern, which it would be useless here to enumerate.

True simplicity excludes likewise from the ornaments of language, all affected brilliance and prettiness of expression. Little conceits in Composition have the same effect as improper condescension in the transactions of life. As in the last case, an exalted character is debased by such a circumstance; so in the first, the highest species of the art is reduced by this affectation in its value, and its author rendered little and contemptible. Ovid, among all the ancients, appears to have fallen most frequently into this fault. The most dignified personages in his fable, are tainted with this bias of the poet. Thus

Phœbus

Phœbus in his addrefs to Phaeton, though interefted as a father to diffuade him from a ruinous attempt, and fpeaking with fervent affection, yet ufes this low kind of wit (as Addifon juftly calls it) by which, fuppofing the ftory to be true, he muft have greatly funk in the reader's eftimation:

Si mutabile pectus
Sit tibi, *conciliis*, non curribus utere noftris.
Met. lib. ii.

In the ftory of Narciffus, the fame affectation characterifeth his defcription. When the youth, heated in the chafe, retires to quench his thirft at the cooling fountain, and firft beholds with admiration and love his own beautiful face, the poet defcribes his firft emotions by faying,

Dum fitim fedare cupit; fitis altera crevit;

" while he ftrived to quench one thirft he raifed another," i. e. the thirft of gazing with confuming defire on his own beauty. Thefe childifh quibbles which the author defigned for ornaments to this (otherwife) noble poem, are incompatible with that fimplicity which is conftituted by a natural

tural though happy difpofition of the fitteft words, conveying ideas to the mind with eafe and perfpicuity.

As we are here, however, confidering the illuftrations of difcourfe, which are not carried on in the preceding examples, we fhall felect one other paffage from this poet, in which he endeavours to heighten our idea of diftrefs by comparifon. When Hypermneftra, in one of his Epiftles, defcribes her terror upon having heard the groans of her murdered kindred, and when fhe trembled every moment for the life of her hufband, fhe expreffeth her emotions by faying,

> Ut leni zephyro fragiles vibrantur ariftæ;
> Frigida populeas ut quatit aura comas;
> Aut fic, aut etiam tremui magis *.————

" As

---

* Epift. Heroid. p. 136. Edit. Delph. Though the writings of Ovid abound with little faults of the kind here pointed out, yet thefe are eafily excufed when we find them abounding likewife with fuch examples of genuine fublimity, of picturefque defcription, of happy felection, and of juft and beautiful illuftration, as muft convince every reader that the author poffeffed an eminent fhare of the moft exalted qualities of the human mind. His account, or rather prophecy

"As fragile reeds vibrate to the gentle
"zephyr; as the leaves of the poplar
"quiver

---

prophecy of the general conflagration in the first book of his Metamorphosis, affords a well known instance of sublimity.

Esse quoque in fatis reminiscitur affore tempus, &c.

In the succeeding book, when Phaeton has thrown all nature in confusion, by having mismanaged the chariot of the Sun (a thought which a great imagination could alone have conceived) there is a circumstance selected with peculiar propriety in the attitude of Tellus rearing her blasted head, and addressing Jupiter in her last resource. The poet, after having painted the universal conflagration, makes this personage arise from the center of her dark dominions. But no sooner does she face the light, than, before she can utter a word, we are told

 Opposuit manum fronti, magnoque tremore
 Omnia concutiens, *paullum subsedit,* & infra
 Quam solet esse fuit.—   Met. lib. ii.

The circumstance of her clapping her hand upon her head as soon as she felt the heat, is natural and picturesque; but when we observe her shrinking immediately after, and seeking a cooler seat before she can speak, we admire the address and genius of the poet, who by this single stroke impresseth a stronger idea of the universal ruin that threatened nature, than by any description however elaborate. An imagination truly of a superior order is never evinced more conspicuously, than by fixing on one circumstance vividly characteristical, instead of running into minute representation. In the fine poem entitled Carthon, Ossian

represents

" quiver to the gale—I trembled thus, and
" even more."—Surely this image is unnatural and affected. A person animated by some part of the feelings which the recollection of so tremendous a scene must have awakened, would never have used any metaphor whatever to express the convulsion of agonized nature, and far less one borrowed from objects which are shown in the sport and wantonness of fancy.

The most perfect examples of simplicity in the images with which the style of Composition ought to be embellished, are to be found in the sacred writings. Of a far different kind from the instances formerly mentioned, is the Evangelist's description of the scene presented to the astonished spectators who went on the third day to visit the sepulchre of our Saviour!—

---

represents the ruins of Balelutha in the same manner, by the figure of " a fox looking out at a window." This power of calling out a variety of ideas exhibiting a complete representation of many objects, by the selection of one single stroke, characteriseth genius in its utmost extent, and is rarely to be found unless in works of the greatest eminence.

" Behold!

"Behold! there was a great earthquake! For the angel of the Lord defcended from heaven, and came, and rolled back the ftone from the door, and fat on it!— His countenance was like lightning! and his raiment white as fnow! And for fear of him the keepers did fhake, and became as dead men!" Let any reader of the leaft fenfibility, compare the feelings excited by this defcription with thofe that are rouzed by the preceding one. The tranfaction is related fo fimply as to betray no affectation in the writer: yet we fee the ftone removed from the fepulchre, behold the face and appearance of him who fat on it; and fhake with the guard who were chilled with amazement at the fcene!

An effect very different from the former is produced by the following paffage; yet the fame unaffected eafe and fimplicity of illuftration give its fignificance to each. When the Gods are engaged in combat with each other, upon winding up the ftory of the Iliad, Neptune and Apollo advance with an hoftile femblance, and the god

god of ocean dares his compeer with some pride and superiority to the fight. The dignity of both characters is here to be preserved; and Homer has succeeded wonderfully in keeping up the majesty of the divine nature in the conduct of Apollo while he retires from Neptune. Neither arrogating equality with, nor acknowledging inferiority to the other, he only shows, by an image which has peculiar significance in the mouth of a deity, that the subject of their dispute is not of importance enough to justify their contention.

Εννοσιγαι, ουκ αν με σαοφρονα μυθησαιο
Εμμεναι, ει δη σοι γε, βροτων ενεκα πολεμιζω
Δειλων, οι φυλλοισιν εοικοτες, αλλοτε μεν τε
Ζαφλεγεες τελεθουσιν αρουρης καρπον εδοντες,
Αλλοτε δ'αυ φθινυθουσιν ακηριοι.

—— To combat for mankind
Ill suits the wisdom of celestial mind.
For what is man?—Calamitous by birth,
They owe their life and nourishment to earth;
Like yearly leaves that now with beauty crown'd
Smile on the sun, now wither on the ground. POPE.

The comparison which the mind is led by this passage to form betwixt the glorious Being who pronounceth these words,

and

and the creatures to whom they refer, ineffably heightens the effect produced by them. What can be conceived more remote from the immutable essence of Deity than leaves scattered on earth by the gales of autumn!—Yet what more expressive of the fragility of man!

III. We have now considered simplicity as a character of just Composition, extending to every species of this comprehensive art, and not only consistent with, but required necessarily to constitute the principal beauties we admire in it.—But the question will here naturally occur,—by what method is this excellence to be acquired?—In answer to this enquiry, let it be observed, that difficult as such an imitation of nature may be deemed in most instances, yet it is often hit off most happily by those who appear to have aimed least at its attainment. He who thoroughly comprehends his subject, and who is attentive rather to that kind of expression which a sentiment requires, than to those superfluous ornaments which may set it off to advantage, will probably convey it

in

in the simpleft and moft natural language *. A mind in which the underftanding exerts confiderable influence, will permit the language to rife with the thought (if we may thus exprefs it), rather than the thought to be exalted by the expreffion; as the words in this cafe will always be fuitable, and every object will be fhown in *full*, but not in *ftrained* dimenfions. Thus the fublime, the rational, the picturefque, the pathetic, will each exert its *proper* influence on the mind; producing that effect which nature, happily imitated, never fails to accomplifh. When, on the contrary, a fuperficial fentiment is elaborately decorated with the pomp of ornamental epithet, a judicious reader is fenfible, upon recollection, that the part is overacted; and challenges immediately the defect of fimplicity. A difproportion appears betwixt the thought ftript of its ornaments, and the words that

---

* " Confperfa fit oratio (fays Cicero) verborum fententiarumque floribus, id non fufum per totam orationem, fed ita diftinctum, ut fint quafi in ornatu infignia quædam difpofita & lumina." De Orat. lib. iii.

convey it, which indicates a correfponding difproportion of thofe powers which gave rife originally to fo unnatural an affemblage.

A certain pedantic affectation may characterife the ftyle of an author's compofition as much as it may his manners. In both cafes a reader of penetration will impute this fault to the fame caufe, a ftriking defect of the difcerning faculty. Both therefore may be corrected by the. fame means. Eafe and elegance of addrefs is obtained by frequenting the beft company, and by converfing with people whom thefe popular qualities have rendered univerfally agreeable. By thefe means the ruft of pedantry is gradually filed off, and a man without having practifed flavifh imitation, becomes affimilated to thofe whom he hath regarded as models, while his deportment ftill continues to be marked by thofe radical fignatures, in their full ftrength, which nature ftamps as indelibly on the mind as on the countenance. In Compofition we ought to proceed in a fimilar manner. By entering deeply into meta-

metaphyfical fpeculation, a man who wants that acutenefs of intellect, that power of developing truth from the chaos of abftracted definition and plaufible diftinction, which denominates a mafter in this fcience, will catch the faults of his original without acquiring his excellence. One philofopher who thinks deeply, but whofe difpofition is accurate and his language perfpicuous, will acquire imitators, who, unable to enter with real difcernment into a fubject, puzzle themfelves and their readers by a conftant affectation of precifion; and, incapable of ranging diftinct objects with accuracy, throw a promifcuous glare over all. By this abfurd attempt the genuine character of the imitator is *diftorted* (if we may thus exprefs it), but not *concealed:*—an inequality which might have been overlooked is only called out into confpicuous light by comparifon, and we fee not what the man was defigned for by nature, but what he is rendered by attempting to be more.

In order, therefore, to exprefs our thoughts at the fame time with precifion and simplicity, a writer ought to peruse the most approved standards in every literary department, but without a settled purpose to follow invariably any original whatever. His own manner will form insensibly while he is engaged in studying those of others which have obtained approbation; and that discriminating bias which cannot be *concealed*, will be set off to advantage by being shown undisguised. There is an affectation even of *ease*, which to a man of true sensibility is obvious and disgusting. Like the aukward gestures of a pedant affecting to imitate elegance of manners, the real character appears every moment through the disguise, and a distorted resemblance exposeth it to ridicule [*]. It is by studying the writings of authors, who themselves have followed the standard of nature, that we shall obtain that expres-

---

[*] In order to have this observation exemplified, an ingenious reader may compare the writings of Addison (one of the easiest of authors) with some more modern performances. The flowing and elegant language of the former forms a contrast to stiffness and affectation, which shows these in a point of view more conspicuous than when they are contemplated apart.

sion

sion appropriated to every object so happily as to admit of no alteration without being injured, which we understand by the term *simple*. A taste naturally good may be spoiled by being conversant only with faulty and defective models, and a judgment which would have despised those little conceits that sometimes stand in place of interesting sentiment, may be brought to approve and even imitate these, when characterising the patterns that are submitted to its examination.

SECTION III.

Of Perspicuous Composition.

IT is a truth at the same time suggested by reflection, and confirmed by the concurring testimony of all authors who have thought on the subject of Composition, that one character which ought to distinguish principally every species of it without exception, is a certain happy perspicuity. This excellence goes under different names, as the subjects direct to which it is applied *. An ancient critic, who considers perspicuity in as extensive a view as we are required to take upon this occasion, explains its meaning so pro-

---

* Quintilian denominates perspicuity the capital excellence of an orator. " Prima est (says he) eloquentiæ virtus perspicuitas." Lib. iii. c. 3. But he immediately explains himself. " Quo quisque ingenio minus valet, hac (perspicuitate) se magis attollere, & dilatare conatur, ut statura breves in digitos eriguntur, & plura infirmi minantur." Id. ibid. This would appear at first to be an inadequate view of the present subject, which cannot, as we shall see afterwards, distinguish, at least in one important sense, the writings of an author who has a small share of genius. Sometimes this word is used to signify philosophical evidence. Thus Diogenes Laertius defines it. Σαφηνεια δε εςι λεξις γνωριμως παριςωσα το νοουμενον. Ζεν. βιβ. ζ. The great critic, to whom we have often had recourse, gives a general definition of perspicuity which exhibits a full view of it when applied to all subjects. Διαφανες δε λεγω ο εςι μεν ορατον, ου καθ' αυτο δε ορατον ως απλως ειπειν, αλλα δε αλλοτριον χρωμα. Περι ψυχ. βιβ. β. κεφ. ζ. That vivid representation (so different from the perspicuity of philosophy) which distinguisheth the poet and the orator, and which may be said to constitute this character in their spheres, is included in this definition. The medium by which it is obtained, is language properly selected.

perly

perly in his general eſtimate, that in order clearly to comprehend its uſe and to diſcover the method of obtaining it, we ſhall ſelect ſuch of his thoughts as are connected moſt nearly with the plan of this eſſay. " Perſpicuity of diſcourſe is con-
" ſtituted by the union of purity or ſim-
" plicity, and accuracy. The firſt of
" theſe (he obſerves) includes all the forms
" of eloquence he had formerly treated
" of;—ſentiment, the manner of diſcuſſing
" a ſubject, expreſſion, &c. But accuracy,
" ευκρινεια (as he calls it), relates principally
" to the ſecond of theſe;—the method in
" which a ſubject is treated. Thoſe ſen-
" timents or propoſitions, which may be
" denominated pure, are ſuch as either
" are or ſeem to be common to all in ge-
" neral, and to have nothing in them con-
" cealed or abſtracted."—Of theſe he produceth examples.

Purity is here taken in its moſt enlarged ſenſe, as diſtinguiſhing the ſentiment as well as the ſtyle of Compoſition: and it is unqueſtionably true, that this character of the art here treated of, is obtained in the greateſt

greatest perfection by him, who not only treats in such a manner of common subjects as to render his sentiments universally intelligible, but who has the art of explaining intricate theories so clearly as to make every idea appear obvious and familiar. This most probably is our author's meaning *. He proceeds to say; that " the method of treating a subject
" has the nearest affinity to that purity
" which has been explained. A discourse
" is distinguished by both, when the au-
" thor plainly relates a fact; and pro-
" ceeding to speak of some truth nakedly
" laid open, introduceth no foreign cir-
" cumstance into his narration †. By
foreign

---

* Should we suppose him to have meant that purity is inconsistent with abstraction or subtlety of ideas, the observation would not be just. Perspicuity relates not to the nature of objects, but to the dress in which these are pourtrayed. It obtains when objects of whatever kind are distinctly placed before the mind; and it is violated when these are detailed inaccurately. The objects themselves are of no consequence.

† Σαφηνειαν τοινυν λογε ποιει Ευκρινεια και καθαροτης. Γινεται δε ΚΑΘΑΡΟΣ μεν λογος απασι χεδον τοις προειρημενοις, εννοια, μεθοδω, λεξει, και τοις λοιποις.

foreign circumstances here, are meant such as are forced in unnaturally without being related to the principal subject. An heterogeneous combination of this kind renders a discourse inexplicable, and is indeed incompatible both with justness of sentiment, and with perspicuity of expression. That we may do justice to this important branch of our present enquiry, we shall consider perspicuity as a character of just Composition—as discovered in the general disposition of any subject whatever, particularly of one that is comprehensive and complicated:—as appearing with peculiar propriety in abstracted philosophical disquisition:—and as characterising, in a sense higher and more animated than the former, the most perfect productions of poetry and eloquence.

λοιποις. Ευκρινεια δε το μεν πλεισον εχει περι του μεθοδου.—Εννοιαι εισι καθαραι αι κοιναι παντων, και εις απαντας ανελθουσαι, η δοξασαι απελθειν βαρεις αφ' εαυτων ουσαι, και γνωριμοι, και μηδεν εχουσαι βαθυ, μηδε περινοημενον. ΕΡΜΟΓΕΝ. περι ΙΔΕΩΝ τομ. πρωτ. τμημ. Γ.

I. We have in a preceding part of this essay, endeavoured to explain at considerable length the use of method in general, and to take a view of the *understanding* as wholly occupying this extensive province. In the present, beyond all other employments, judgment may evince the clearness or obscurity of its original conceptions. It hath been formerly observed, that in every species of Composition, without exception, a method either concealed or obvious is always carried on, and that while another faculty may superintend the execution distinguished by no regularity of procedure; *this* in every rational mind maintains a certain harmony and proportion, or attempts to maintain these, difficult as it sometimes is to observe its operations.

The general plan of a work is said to be perspicuous when it is such as fully comprehends the subject to be treated of; and when the subordinate parts though having each its proper tendency to promote an ultimate purpose, yet coincide not

Observations on Composition.

in such a manner as to render the disposition perplexed, but are placed precisely in the most natural arrangement. When an author takes a large compass in his work, and proposeth to include in it a very diversified series of objects, it becomes necessary to form a certain general and methodised estimate of the whole, of whose fitness and comprehension the reader may pronounce without having entered into minute investigation. It is, however, an high recommendation to a performance in many instances, that the method is concealed (when materials less diversified present themselves) and that it opens gradually with new light upon the mind, as a reader is led in this manner imperceptibly and agreeably from one step to another, and never comprehends the full process of reasoning until he arrives at the end of it. Nor in the conduct of an extensive plan is perspicuity violated by the use of *digressions*, even though we may be unable at first to perceive in these the most distant relation to the point in view. When an author disentangles himself

agreeably

agreeably from a little embarrassment of this nature (as it may be judged), and either elucidates his argument, or renders it entertaining, or accomplisheth both ends at once by this medium, we justly form a favourable opinion of his judgment; and the sentiment is impressed on memory more powerfully in proportion as its illustration was unexpected.—Let us try an example.

In the noble dialogue on the immortality of the soul, entitled Phedon, Socrates, after having endeavoured to prove his point by arguments drawn from the doctrine of contraries giving rise to each other*, and after having likewise attempted to view the soul in its supposed state of pre-existence †,

---

* His argument is this. All things (says he) are produced by their contraries. Beauty, for instance, is opposite to deformity, justice to injustice. What is called less, must have been reduced to that state from greater magnitude:—swiftness in the same manner ariseth from debility, and strength from weakness. Now if every thing ariseth thus from its contrary,—what, says Socrates to his friends, does life give rise to?—Death. What then must death breed?—Unquestionably—Life. Φαιδ. τμημ. ιε. ιϛ.

† Id. Τμημ. ιη. &c.

at last comes to show that it is an immaterial substance. He illustrates this doctrine, as usual, by comparison. "The
" real essence of things (says he) equality,
" beauty, &c. while external objects are
" constantly varying, is any change
" wrought upon these?—There is none,
" his friends reply. What then, says
" the philosopher, shall we pronounce of
" beautiful objects, as men, horses, gar-
" ments, &c. are these opposite to the
" former in this sense, that by no method
" whatever can they be kept in their ori-
" ginal state?—These, it is answered, are
" always fluctuating.—Of those two then
" (resumes Socrates, after having reasoned
" at length on the subject) which does
" the soul seem most to resemble, the di-
" vine, or the mortal;—the perishable,
" or the immutable?—The mind, say his
" friends, we must acknowledge resem-
" bles what is unchangeable, and our
" body what is mortal*."—By the little
circum-

---

* Αυτη η ΟΥΣΙΑ ης λογον διδομεν του ειναι και
ερωτωντες και αποκρινομενοι, ποτερον οσαυτως αει εχει
κατα

circumlocution employed here, Socrates' meaning appears perfectly obvious, and his reasoning at the same time is strengthened and elucidated. Another beautiful stroke of the same kind the reader will find in the note *.

Though

κατα ταυτα η αλλοτ' αλλως; αυτο το ΙΣΟΝ, αυτο το ΚΑΛΟΝ, αυτο Εκαςον ο εςι το ΟΝ, μηποτε μεταβολην και ηντινουν ενδεχεται.—Ωσαυτως, εφη, αναγκη, ο Κεβης, και κατα τα αυτα εχειν· τι δε των πολλων καλων οιον ανθρωπων, η ιππων, η ιματιων, η αλλων ωντινωνουν τοιητων—αρα κατα τα αυτα εχει, η παν τουναντιον εκεινοις, υτε αυτα αυτοις υτε αλληλοις υδεποτε ως επος ειπειν, υδαμως κατα ταυτα εςιν; Ουτως αυ εφη ταυτα ο Κεβης υδεποτε ωσαυτως εχει.—Και κατα ταυτα, αυ ποτερον σοι δοκει ομοιον τω ΘΕΙΩ ειναι, και ποτερον τω ΘΝΗΤΩ ;—Δηλαδη, ω Σωκρατες οτι η μεν ΨΥΧΗ τω ΘΕΙΩ, το δε ΣΩΜΑ τω ΘΝΗΤΩ. ΠΛΑΤ. Φαιδ. τμημ. κε. κη.

* When Simmias and Cebes, in the same dialogue, have proposed such arguments against the immortality of the soul as staggered all the hearers, and appeared to overthrow all that Socrates had advanced, we are told he kept silence for some time, and observing the impression made upon his audience, prepared them to expect that he would clear up their doubts by a little piece of conduct adapted with admirable propriety to the occasion. Instead of making any direct answer to the objections, stroking Phedon's head, who sat by him,

Though however, circumstances apparently digressive are thus advantageous in general to perspicuity, yet in conducting the plan of a work, an author ought to avoid the fault of extending these to any disproportioned length. When this is the case, we necessarily either lose sight of the

---

him, and playing with the ringlets of his hair,—
" To-morrow perhaps, said he, Phedon, you will poll
" away these beautiful locks.—It will probably be so,
" replied he. Not, said Socrates, if you take my
" advice.—Why?—To-day both you and I will per-
" form this office upon ourselves, if our argument is
" indeed lost without hope of recovery." By this beautiful digression (referring to the Argives, who cut their hair and made a vow not to let it grow until they had conquered the Spartans) he at the same time teacheth his hearers not to be daunted by the plausibility of objections, however strong, at first view, until these have been scanned deliberately; and relieves the mind, fatigued with attention, to abstracted reasoning, and requiring a pause to return to it with alacrity. The subject is here likewise introduced with great advantage, as it comes in some measure unexpectedly; and before the philosopher speaks, we conceive him equal to the solution we desire from him. Circumstances of this kind, happily introduced and properly conducted, indicate great knowledge of human nature, and a discernment well adapted to the purposes that ought to be accomplished by philosophical research.

original

original defign, or purfue it with difficulty; and a performance in which the thoughts taken feparately may be clearly expreffed, will appear as a whole to be compofed of broken and detached parts without fymmetry or coherence. In the fphere of Compofition, as in that of converfation, a man who rambles in his narration or in his reafoning, without keeping fome principal object clofely and invariably in his view is juftly cenfured, as deficient in clearnefs of intellectual perception, and as fhooting without any determinate aim. As, therefore, to take in, and to range in perfpicuous order, the various parts of a complicated fubject demands comprehenfion, fo to purfue this order clearly, when once eftablifhed, through all its branches, a power is requifite of fixing the intellectual eye upon fucceffive objects fo fteadily, as that the more may never prevent us from doing juftice to the lefs important; and that from impatience to arrive at a favourite topic, we may not hurry too lightly over fuch as convey not, when contemplated, fo high a degree of pleafure. The firft first of these powers cannot be carried by any application beyond certain limits, extended or contracted according to the original strength or debility of the faculties of the mind:—the other may be exerted by any man of moderate understanding, who has resolution to fix his thought, as he may do the external organ of sight, upon any object whatever, until he gains an habit of viewing it deliberately, and of delineating it with precision.

A series of objects thus passing successively in review before the mind, will by these means be ranged in perspicuous order, and as in a family managed with well-regulated œconomy, where attention not distracted by many promiscuous employments, is bestowed on each at the proper season; so here the parts will stand together by this steady recollection, in such disposition as to give an air of consistency and proportion to the whole. When the first draught of a work is completed in this manner, and the principal parts sketched out, the inferior members fall naturally into their places, each occu-

pying

pying that to which it is beſt adapted. Nothing therefore, further remains to render a diſcourſe perſpicuous in every ſenſe of that expreſſion, than that the language ſhould ſtand in the ſame relation to the ſentiments which theſe laſt maintain reciprocally to each other. This likewiſe will follow in a great meaſure, as a conſequence from the principles here eſtabliſhed. A man is ſeldom at a loſs to convey ideas clearly to others, which he diſtinctly apprehends himſelf. When we are at a loſs for words upon any occaſion to render our meaning explicit, this embarraſſment generally ariſeth from ſome defective view of our ſubject, or from ſome combination of ſimilar ideas, which we cannot eaſily diſcriminate. Let a man thoroughly comprehend, and be deeply intereſted in any buſineſs; he will then expreſs himſelf with energy and fluency. His language however inaccurate, will have ſtrong ſignificance, and he will impart to others thoſe ſenſations with vivacity, which have made a forcible and permanent impreſſion on himſelf.

II. The

II. The perspicuity here recommended, though it is an essential character of Composition, without which no species of it can be either entertaining or instructive, yet ought in no case to be studied with closer attention, than when the mind investigates remote and abstracted propositions. It is exceedingly difficult, when we attempt to carry to its utmost limits the power by which that point is perceived, where truth and falshood are first disunited; to distinguish from each other objects almost perfectly similar so nicely, as that plausible may not be substituted in place of essential difference; and apparent be received as real information. We may judge of truth and error as of empires whose boundaries are not accurately specified :—when we have made considerable progress in the precincts of the last without intention, we may suspect ourselves to have wandered from the right path, and may attempt to regain it. But while this deviation is a matter of uncertainty, reflection only serves to augment our embarrassment, and we can form no just and satisfactory conclusion. Thus it is too often with intellectual research, when carried beyond the limits which perspicuous investigation would prescribe. Whether this practice of perplexing what we mean to elucidate, ariseth from the desire of establishing just principles upon the most solid foundation, from the hope of subduing difficulty by perseverence, or (what is most common) from the vanity of building new theories, and of exploding former systems of belief, merely perhaps because these have had universal influence;—from whichever of these causes derived, it is certain, that the understanding is here made the dupe of the passions in many instances, by whose influence men having been persuaded to overleap the bounds assigned to the researches of reason, have involved themselves in the inextricable labyrinth of error.

In order to avoid being misled in this manner, a man who is solicitous to know how far his sentiments are just, and to render these perspicuous, ought to try whether his ideas will stand the test of
com-

Observations on Composition.

comparison, and of illustration particularly from external objects. With regard to the last, whatever falls under the cognizance of the senses (supposing these to be unimpaired) is exposed in a light abundantly conspicuous. Every eye can distinguish with ease perfect symmetry from visible disproportion, and conveys to the mind that sensation of pleasure or pain which each is calculated universally to excite. A sentiment, therefore, a proposition, or a distinction that can receive illustration by an exact comparison with such an object, and still more with such a series, we may pronounce, without hesitation, to have been distinctly comprehended. Of these, on the other hand, that to which no example can be brought perfectly to correspond; which demands a certain peculiarity of phrase, or is founded wholly in some ambiguous and unexceptionable epithet; ought to be suspected as either having no real existence, or, if it have, as not being thoroughly understood.

When a truth is indeed either self-evident, or is clearly derived from certain general

general principles, examples are superfluous, and can anfwer no purpofe. When again the former is of fuch a nature as to exclude direct comparifon with external objects, fome real, though diftant point of refemblance may be felected; or fome mode of illuftration, drawn from other fources, carried on which, may be adapted to fhow it in the happieft point of view. But whatever purpofe an author may propofe to accomplifh, that of inftruction is at an end as foon as his principles will no longer bear to be enforced in this manner, or are underftood fo defectively that it is not attempted.

Thefe general obfervations on the perfpicuity of philofophical fentiment, will affift us in forming fome judgment of the mode of expreffion that is beft adapted to convey it. On this branch of our fubject it is indeed impoffible to lay down particular rules; becaufe whatever method a writer may purfue, he will always fail of rendering that clear to his readers which is not fully and diftinctly comprehended by himfelf. As the firft ftep, therefore, to acquire

acquire this happy characteristic of Composition, an author must be thoroughly acquainted with the nature and quality of his materials, which he will thus know in what manner to digest. When this important part of his work is over, like an able artist, whose tools are prepared and at hand, he will proceed to put each to that use for which it was originally fitted. To drop the metaphor here, the author ought to consider in what dress thoughts following each other succeffively in the mind, require to be pourtrayed with the fairest prospect of being universally intelligible *. To those who are not internally blind, there is a language that will set off sentiment, even in the most abstracted enquiry, to great advantage, in the same manner as there is a colour or fashion suited with propriety to every complexion. In general, this may be said to lie in that

---

* This is agreeable to Quintilian's clear and accurate account of the manner in which Composition is carried on. "Paulatim res facilius se ostendent, verba respondebunt; compositio sequetur. Cuncta denique ut in familia bene instituta in officio erunt."

simplicity which though confiftent with ftrength, fublimity, pathos, and elegance, yet preferves always the juft medium betwixt abundance and defect *.

But as in the more abftracted difquifitions of philofophy, obfcurity is the fault of all others to be moft feduloufly avoided, and perfpicuity the characteriftic to be principally ftudied, we fhall here lay down a few rules by an exact obfervation of which the attainment of this important purpofe may be facilitated.

1. An author ought then particularly to confider, as foon as he enters upon a work of this kind, by what means a feries of thought, naturally cold and uninterefting, may be rendered as agreeable as poffible; and by what method of procedure an impreffion may be made moft fuccefsfully on that intellectual power to which his difcourfe is principally addreffed. Before a theory, recommended by its novelty as well as truth, can be thoroughly eftablifhed, an author, however diftinguifhed

---

* Sect. ii. p. 23.

by originality, will find that many known truths must be repeated, because the greatest discoveries, when searched to the bottom, arise wholly from principles universally acknowledged, combined in such a manner as may lead to some unexpected conclusion.—Of these even the most superficial may appear with some measure of significance, when the words or *colour* most justly appropriated to it are happily selected. When again this propriety is not attended to as much in the expression of obvious as of abstracted ideas, the *connection* is lost, at least to many readers; and a performance in which these last may be clearly explained, will thus be chargeable upon the whole with obscurity. The writer, therefore, should always remember, that whatever may be his own character, those of his readers are greatly diversified. When his purpose is only to give information to the understanding, this faculty will point out to him the necessity of attending to those which guard (if that expression may be used) the avenues that lead to it. For this purpose he will attend as closely as possible, not only to the strain of his composition in general, but to that peculiar expression which the parts, taken separately, demand as most suitable. Thus he will sometimes (as his judgment may direct) study ease and elegance of phrase; at others, a style more forcible and animated: a part will here require a little heightening when the thought is remote, or the argumentation protracted; and by thus varying his composition judiciously, as his subject becomes diversified, he will obtain the end of rendering his sentiments intelligible, and their impression permanent.

2. As a means still further to promote perspicuity in that kind of disquisition where this acquirement is at the same time most expedient and difficult, a man of understanding will find it necessary to make use, as much as possible, of such words as are most obvious and universally understood. In the present case, such a man will be careful as much of rendering his sentiments obvious and pleasing, as in another he would be of his external appearance.

ance. He whose aspect is not inviting, endeavours naturally to compensate for this inconvenience by the smile of complaisance, elegance of dress, and insinuating manners. We would judge strangely of him, if instead of attempting thus to palliate circumstances that create disgust, we should find him, on the contrary, studiously heightening it by a deportment distant and gloomy as his countenance. It is in the same manner wholly improper to clothe propositions, not easily comprehended, in words which, though familiar to some ears, are unintelligible to others; because obscurity is the consequence of this practice in many instances, when there is otherwise no perplexity either in the disposition, or language of a performance; and readers are discouraged from engaging in a pursuit by this circumstance, which might otherwise have been followed both with pleasure and information.

"What then!—Is the philosopher, the "man of science, exalted far *above the* "*level of his kind* by study, capacity, and "investigation;—is he required to debase

the

" the nobleſt of all acquiſitions, by the uſe
" of inelegant and vulgar phraſeology!
" Ought not ſentiments calculated only
" for the *few*, to be expreſſed in words
" ſuited to their dignity, without regard
" to thoſe for whom they are not..calcu-
" lated *!"—Odi prophanum vulgus &
arceo,

---

* In very early ages it ſeems to have been the practice of philoſophers to conceal their tenets from the cognizance of the vulgar. Hence the Ægyptian hieroglyphics, ſaid to have been invented by Hermes Triſmegiſtus, came to be uſed as expreſſive of certain myſterious doctrines. Theſe, as divine truths, (according to a maxim of Hippocrates) were only to be communicated to men employed in ſacred offices. Pythagoras (the firſt man who aſſumed the name of philoſopher, vide Cicer. Tuſcul. Queſt. lib. v. c. 3. & Diogen. Laert. in proem.) divided his diſciples into two claſſes, the initiated, and the prophane or uninſtructed, and to theſe he adopted his method of teaching. To the former his principles were explained in the cleareſt manner. To the latter, ſymbols and ænigmas were made uſe of. The celebrated maxim, Ἐςι δε παντων χαλεπωτατον ιγκρατευμα τῳ γλωττης κρατειν, recorded by Jamblichus, and the ſilence enjoined to his diſciples, that they might learn to know its importance, were probably deſigned by this celebrated philoſopher to inſtruct his followers in the duty of maintaining impenetrable ſecrecy with regard to certain myſteries, and of digeſting properly thoſe truths

arceo, is the language of this apoſtrophe. To thoſe who uſe it, we would obſerve, that

truths which were to form the ſubjects of their inſtructions. That Pythagoras never propoſed to keep up this ſtyle of obſcurity upon all occaſions, muſt be obvious from the effects which his doctrines are ſaid to have produced upon almoſt all claſſes of mankind. When he travelled through Italy, we are informed by one author, that he made many good as well as learned men, two in particular (Zeleucus and Charondas) eminent lawgivers. Diogen. Laert. lib. viii. By another, that he civilized nations, reſtored liberty to cities, converted thouſands at once to his philoſophy, and even prevailed on women to give up ſome part of their ornaments. Porphyr. Juſtin. lib. xx. c. 4. This conduct diſcovers knowledge of mankind in a very high degree, and is a proof that Pythagoras meant not to ſcreen his philoſophical tenets behind the veil of myſtery. The language he uſed muſt have been perfectly obvious, and levelled to all capacities, when it produced ſuch effects. The ancients in general, we may obſerve, had reaſon in the early ages of ſcience to affect a myſterious air upon ſome occaſions, as from reverence to their perſons, men were thus induced to hold their doctrines in ſuperior eſtimation. Ignorance (which is ſome ſenſe became here the mother of inſtruction, as ſhe is ſaid to have been of devotion), rendered the vulgar credulous with regard to any pretenſions of men whoſe knowledge produced the happieſt conſequences on ſociety. Thus the barbarous Romans were civilized by Numa, becauſe they believed his laws to have been dictated by a divine Being.

that there is a juſt medium betwixt affected pomp, and real meanneſs of expreſſion, as much as there is of dreſs betwixt the tinſel of a beau, and the rags of a beggar. This medium, in the preſent caſe, lies in ſtudying an eaſy, natural, unforced expreſſion, whoſe ſtrength ought to be proportioned to that of the thought; and in which thoſe ſounding epithets that may have propriety and ſignificance upon other occaſions, ought rarely, if ever, to be admitted.

3. The laſt rule we ſhall here lay down for the attainment of perſpicuity in this province of ſcience, is that an author ought to avoid in it, as much as poſſible, running into tedious and protracted periods. There are, indeed, caſes in which a full and modulated ſentence produceth a very ſtriking effect; and it is, no doubt,

---

Being. The legiſlator appeared with ſuitable dignity, and his inſtitutions were received with reverence. The vanity of mankind was likewiſe artfully flattered by this conduct, as each man believed the leader to ſurpaſs himſelf, not by ſuperior abilities, but by the capricious favour of a divinity.

poſſible

possible to conduct it, when consisting of many members, and including great variety of objects, to a close without violating perspicuous order. Thus in the conclusion of an eloquent discourse, in which some point of importance hath been pressed home upon the mind, and different topics selected for this purpose, it is often highly proper to sum up such as have greatest energy in a well conducted climax, as after having been separately illustrated, their combined influence accomplisheth an interesting purpose. Upon other occasions, the end either of persuasion or of conviction is gained more effectually by enumerating several distinct motives or arguments at once, than by any other expedient; because the mind can feel an effect from all acting with united energy, and concentrating (if we may thus express it) their force in one point; which considered apart from each other, these could never have produced. This happens when collateral evidences and incidental circumstances occur in a discourse, whose significance ariseth from their being contemplated

in

in union. But in the inftance here prefented to us, reflection will immediately convince us, that fuch a procedure is neither neceffary nor proper. When feveral arguments or motives of conduct are placed in one point of view, their influence obvioufly depends on their being univerfally underftood. Each therefore, being comprehended as foon as it is mentioned, the mind proceeds without interruption in its career, feeling at laft the full effect, which all taken together are intended to produce *. But a fentiment whofe truth

we

---

* No writer, either ancient or modern, underftood more thoroughly the force of both the methods of perfuafion and conviction mentioned here, than the illuftrious Roman orator and philofopher. When Africanus (in his fublime vifion of that great leader) informs his defcendant of the immortality of the foul, he puts together feveral circumftances, whofe impreffion is ftrong from being placed before the mind in one view. " Tu vero enitere, & fic habeto. *Te* non effe mortalem, fed *corpus hoc*. Nec enim *Tu* is es quem forma ifta declarat, fed *Mens* cujufque is eft quifque, &c. *Deum* te igitur fcito effe: fiquidem *Deus* eft qui viget, qui fentit, qui meminit, qui prævidet, qui tam regit & moderatur & movet id corpus cui præpofitus eft quam hunc mundum princeps ille Deus; & ut mundum

we do not immediately perceive, and far more a succession of these whose connec-

---

dum ex quadam parte mortalem, ipse Deus æternus, sic fragile corpus animus sempiternus movet." Somn. Scipion. He passeth over, as incidental circumstances, the principal events of the life of Scipio, to whom he addressed himself, that he might hasten to the most momentuous of all.—There is great propriety in this conduct. The illustrious actions of Scipio, placed here in one group, prepare us for the last scene, which otherwise would have made no adequate impression. " Quum autem Carthaginem deleveris, triumphum egeris, Censorque fueris, & obieris Legatus Ægyptum, Syriam, Asiam, Græciam; deligere iterum absens consul bellumque maximum conficies, Numantiam exscindes. Sed quum eris curru in Capitolium invectus *offendes Rempublicam*, &c. *Hic* tu Africane ostendas opportebit patriæ, lumen animi, ingenii, conciliique tui." Ibid.—When, again, he enters into close reasoning, his style is indeed clear and forcible, but concise at the same time, and divested of all superfluity.—" Quod semper movetur æternum est. Quod autem motum affert alicui quodque ipsum agitatur aliunde, quando finem habet motus, vivendi finem habeat necesse est. Solum igitur quod sese movet, quia nunquam deseritur a se nunquam ne moveri quidem desinit. Quinetiam cæteris quæ moventur hic fons, hoc principium est movendi. Principio autem nulla est origo. Nam ex principio oriuntur omnia. Ipsum autem nulla ex re oriri potest. Non enim esset hoc principium quod gigneretur aliunde. Quod si nunquam oritur, nec occidit quidem unquam." Ibid.

tion, though close, is unfolded with difficulty, must be explained with precision, and the embarrassment of protracted periods ought to be avoided when it requires attention to pursue the thread of a subject carried on in few words, and with simple illustrations. While an author goes forward in this accurate manner, adapting his expression and images with exact propriety to their objects, he can never be in hazard of extending his researches beyond the province assigned to reason; and his distinctions, however subtle, will have *that real* (not *nominal*) truth, which a reader of discernment will comprehend with satisfaction.

III. The subject of this section as far as we have yet pursued it, characteriseth the spheres of philosophy and history. When we apply it to poetry and eloquence the word is of higher import, and includes that lively painting which gives peculiar energy to every idea, and greatly heightens its impression. We enter by this means not only into the meaning, but into the spirit of an author, and become spectators of of the scenes that are presented to us. This is, indeed, the capital excellence of those branches of Composition which are ultimately addressed either to the passions or the imagination. Of these (in most cases) the most diversified, and perhaps the most difficult task is assigned to the orator. It is his business to unite perspicuous reasoning with animated and beautiful description. Without the former, the principal purpose of his art must remain unaccomplished, and without the latter, the particular application of his arguments can neither penetrate the heart, nor operate on the conduct. When Quintilian denominates perspicuity the capital excellence of an orator, he must have understood the phrase in the sense here assigned to it. He would not have called that character of the style of Composition the principal one, which he represents as in the power of every mad writer of mean parts, who recommends his performance by this quality, when he can do so by no other. By such an assertion he would have debased an art which he justly explains

plains as one of the nobleft to which the mind of man is adequate. It is therefore evident, that this author takes the term Perfpicuity here in its moft enlarged meaning. He underftands by it, that ENAPΓEIA, as the Greeks call it, that emphatical and animated expreffion, by which an accomplifhed orator, fpeaking to the heart of man, obtains the perfection of his art.

In the province of ethical or didactic poetry, where lefs ornament is required than in any other, this vivid reprefentation is highly ufeful, as it impreffeth a thought at the fame time upon the power of imagination, and that of remembrance. Here however, that it may accomplifh this purpofe, the imagery muft be juft and perfectly appropriated.—" Honourable age (fays the author of the Wifdom of Solomon) is not that which confifteth of a number of years, neither is meafured by length of days. But *wifdom is the grey hairs* to man, and *an unfpotted life is old age.*" This juft and inftructive obfervation acquires a light, and an expreffion ineffably ftriking from the colours here
caft

cast on it which cannot escape a reader of the least sensibility. To say merely that the author's language is perspicuous, in the common sense of that epithet, would be a representation of it extremely inadequate. It is picturesque in an high degree; and we observe a sentiment in its full force expressed in very few words, which might have been expatiated upon to much less purpose through many a period.

The graces of Composition, by whose aid this striking representation is carried on, are indispensably requisite to characterise every other branch of the poetic art. The mind can never be raised to any pitch of enthusiasm, unless the objects that pass successively before it are not clearly, but vividly displayed *. The passions must be wrought into commotion by na-

---

* Δει δε τας μυθας συνιςαναι, και τη λεξει συναπεργαζεσθαι, ότι μαλιςα προς ομματων τιθεμενον. Ουτω γαρ αναργεςατα ορων ωσπερ παρ' αυτας γιγνομενος τοις πραττομενοις, ευρισκοι το πρεπον, και ηκιςα αν λανθανοιτο τα υπεναντια.

ΑΡΙΣΤΟΤ. περι ΠΟΙΗΤ.

tural

tural and pathetic exhibitions; and we speak to the heart only, when circumstances of diftrefs are fo particularly enumerated, and fo juftly painted, as that the reader may be led to feel thefe as his own. It is by no means neceffary to effectuate thefe purpofes, that the ftyle of Compofition fhould always be diftinguifhed by colouring. Arguments forcibly expreffed, facts emphatically related, and appeals to the underftanding or the paffions, drawn from thefe fources, and properly pointed to operate on either, become not only clear, but highly interefting, and accomplifh the ends to which thefe branches of the art are directed.

These general obfervations on perfpicuity, as it relates to poetry and eloquence, it was proper to throw out here, that we might give this fubject its full extent. It will be confidered more particularly when we come to treat of the two arts feparately, as forming important fpecies of the fubject of this effay.

IV. From the remarks we have made on perfpicuous Compofition, it will be

eafier

easier to develope the causes to which the defect of this character ought to be ascribed. These are diversified according to the taste and complexion of the writer. Some men, who possess a comprehensive and penetrating judgment, without an adequate proportion of imagination, bestow so much attention on the sentiment of a performance that they are satisfied when the expression is rendered intelligible to themselves. The human mind is surely viewed by such persons in a very defective light, and we may pronounce that understanding, however comprehensive, to have formed a partial estimate in this instance, which appears to have judged of all others as corresponding exactly to its own standard. An author ought therefore to remember, that few readers are capable of entering as much into the spirit of a work as the writer himself, and that of those who are capable, still fewer will sit down to read merely for instruction, when their attention is not kept awake by the charm of variety. This, indeed, sometimes proceeds from the defect of imagination, and sometimes from not having attended to its real value and importance in the sphere of Composition.

An extreme of any kind is always pernicious, and by running from one into another a man often falls into that very error which he most sedulously studied to avoid. Opposite causes produce, in this instance, the same consequence. As the former of these seem to require that every reader should possess as great a share of judgment, and should bestow as much attention on their writings as they have done themselves, the latter, by taking a course directly contrary, demand of their readers acuteness, discernment, and the quickest sensibility. Authors distinguished by exuberance of imagination, become often obscure by giving too much scope to it, as they are either hurried by it into digressions, whose connection with the principal subject the reader may not be disposed, perhaps may not be capable of tracing with accuracy; or as the natural proportions of an object are concealed by the luxury of its colour. These are faults into which the

the greateſt geniuſes are ſometimes betrayed *.

Another ſet of writers fall into obſcurity by an affectation of conciſeneſs.

―― Brevis eſſe laboro,
Obſcurus fio.   Hor.

It is equally injudicious to croud thoughts together too cloſely, as it is to lengthen out a few into great compaſs by verboſe expreſſion, and tedious declamation. By the firſt method, a general air of obſcurity is caſt upon a work, even when particular objects may be diſtinctly exhibited, juſt as a confuſed idea is excited by a multitude of people ſtanding cloſely together, among whom however the individuals are ſtill diſtinct from each other, and only require to be placed at ſome diſtance. This fault as inconſiſtent with ſimple, as well as with perſpicuous compoſition, we have treated of and exemplified ſo particularly in a

---

* See this ſubject explained more particularly, vol. i. It is illuſtrated at large, with regard to its effects on Compoſition, by an application to the Odes of Pindar, in the author's Eſſay on Lyric Poetry, Let. ii. p. 111. octavo edit.

preceding section, as to render an enlargement here unneceffary *.

The laft, and indeed the moft common fource of obfcurity in Compofition, is the ambition of attempting to perform more than we are able, and fixing on a fubject the parts of which we cannot range in any juft difpofition.

Sumite materiam veftris qui fcribitis æquam
Viribus, & verfate diu quid *ferre recufent,*
Quid *valeant humeri.* Cui *lecta* potenter erit res
Nec facundia deferet hunc, neque lucidus ordo. HOR.

An author who hath paid no proper attention to this rule, muft neceffarily be involved in inextricable difficulties, and his thoughts muft be vague, inaccurate, and undigefted. Many fentiments rifing unformed while the mind takes a view of fome comprehenfive theme, without cool recollection its views are apt to be diftracted, and without compafs inadequate. Like the difcourfes of which Cicero complains among his contemporaries, " no-
" thing in this cafe will occupy its proper
" place. Senfe will be loft amidft the

---
* Sect. i.

" mul-

" multitude of words, and that which
" ought to have conveyed light to the
" mind, will only involve it in obscurity
" or darkness *." He therefore, upon
the whole, who would write with perspicuity, after having methodised his subject, ought to avoid making use either of superfluous, uncommon, or ambiguous expressions. To obtain this character his digressions must be natural, (particularly in the higher species of Composition) his allusions apt, his characters marked with discriminating peculiarities, and his illustrations fitted with exact conformity to their objects.

---

* " Res simulac Fusius aut vester æqualis Pomponius agere cœpit non æque quid dicant nisi admodum attendi intelligo.. Ita confusa est oratio, ita perturbata nihil ut fit primum, nihil ut secundum tantaque insolentia ac turba verborum ut oratio quæ lumen adhibere rebus debet ea obscuritatem & tenebras afferat, ut quodammodo ipsi sibi in dicendo obstrepere videantur." De Orat. lib. iii. cap. 13.

SECTION IV.

Of elegant Composition.

ELEGANT Composition is a phrase applied to writings in which we suppose that there are certain peculiar graces distinguishing the sentiments, and ornamenting the language in which these are conveyed. Under these two heads therefore, we shall consider this character of the art here treated of, that those readers who have used this expression without comprehending thoroughly its import, may be able to distinguish real from apparent elegance, and may appropriate to the word some determinate meaning.

I. It will be acknowledged by every man who bestows any reflection on this subject, that the word Elegance, to whatever objects it may be applied, stands in opposition to rusticity, and rudeness. Whatever is sordid, mean, and vulgar, either in a man's opinion, deportment, or even dress, denominates inelegance when prevailing in any obvious degree; but when

when predominating conspicuously excites disgust and aversion. As the term elegant therefore excludes, in all senses, the coarse and disagreeable from entering into its objects, so the word refinement (a phrase often used without much propriety) denotes the highest proportion of this character, in which so little alloy is to be observed as serves to heighten, rather than debase the object, and throws additional lustre on what is truly beautiful, by the foil that is opposed to it.

Sentiments either in a series of close reasoning, or in looser miscellaneous observation, may be said to have elegance when these are so artfully ranged, and so happily exposed, as to be shown always in the most pleasing point of view. In a discourse levelled against the absurdities, the vices, or the follies of mankind, the ultimate purpose is by no means agreeable; and it is therefore necessary, that prejudices should be attacked with much circumspection in order to be effectually eradicated. Opinions that are riveted by time,

time, and habits that have been ftrengthened by indulgence, cannot be fuccefsfully combated, unlefs the arguments by whofe ufe it is propofed to imprefs conviction on the underftanding, are enforced by circumftances that foothe and attack the imagination. In this procefs it is obvious, that one falfe ftep will overturn a whole fyftem, and will induce the mind to reject it as abfurdity. Inftead of liftening with impartiality to the fpeaker or the writer on fuch an occafion, we are difpofed, on the contrary, either to fearch out miftakes and fallacies in his reafoning, or to fupport our own fentiments, however irrational, by calling argument to the affiftance of paffion. For as it is an eafy matter to convince or to deceive reafon by plaufible appearances when the paffions are once interefted againft it, fo it is, on the other hand, extremely difficult to gain the approbation of the former of thefe, without at the fame time influencing the latter. Both can then only be brought to concur in one fentiment, when thoughts are combined

bined in such arrangement as that the unpleasing part is cast into a shade, and the most beautiful side is exposed to view. Elegance of sentiment must distinguish every work in which this purpose is accomplished. Gentle and insinuating eloquence; steals into the heart upon such an occasion, and disposeth us to listen to the person, by whom we are addressed, by establishing a prepossession in his favour.

1. This purpose is accomplished in some cases, when, instead of addressing roughly an individual, stimulated by the impulse of a ruling passion, he is led, by general observations apparently levelled at no particular object, to see the effects that arise from indulging it. A beautiful example of this kind occurs in the Iliad. When the Greeks are just returned dispirited from an unsuccessful battle, and their leader, either as an expression of his own sentiments, or as a trial of theirs, proposeth to leave their conquest uncompleted; Diomed replies, with an insolence and ferocity deserving a severe reprimand. After having accused the prince of pusillanimity and

and cowardice, he profeffeth his own delight in war, and his refolution to continue himfelf before Troy, though all the other Greeks fhould defert it. Neftor with great propriety attempts to cool this ardour. But inftead of directly reprimanding a young hero, fired by a fuppofed injury, and impatient of reproof, he, on the contrary, elegantly compliments him on the freedom and boldnefs of his addrefs; and after having thus put him in good humour, artfully throws in the following reflection.

Αφρητωρ' αθεμιστος, ανεστιος εστιν εκεινος,
Ος πολεμου εραται, επιδημιου, οκρυοεντος. ΙΛΙΑΔ. I.
Curs'd is the man, and void of law and right,
Unworthy property, unworthy light,
Unfit for public rule, or private care,
That wretch, that monfter, who delights in war. POPE.

There is great delicacy in this conduct, as the paffions by which Diomed would have been blinded are laid afleep; and his reafon is at leifure to perceive and to apply in its full force the fucceeding obfervation. It is from fuch inftances as thefe, that the eloquence of Neftor, in the Iliad,

is

is said by Quintilian to be characterised by a sweetnefs inexpreffibly pleafing *.

In the fine addrefs of Cæfar to the Roman fenate, whom he would have perfuaded to pardon Cataline, we meet with a fimilar inftance of fentiment elegantly applied, not merely to influence the conduct of an individual, but to regulate the determination of an illuftrious affembly. On the part of Cæfar great addrefs was here peculiarly requifite, becaufe the caufe in which he fpoke was univerfally odious, and becaufe he himfelf was fufpected to have been engaged in the confpiracy. Knowing, therefore, that his audience was equally prejudiced againft the confpirators and their advocate, he introduceth his difcourfe with fome general obfervations defigned to ftrike at thefe prejudices without giving offence to individuals.—" All " men, fays he, confcript fathers, who " confult about dubious affairs, ought to " judge of thefe with a difpaffionate

---

* " Ex ore Neftoris dixit dulciorem melle profluere fermonem, qua certe delectatione nihil fingi majus poteft." Lib. xii. c. 10.

" temper,

"temper, uninfluenced equally by anger, "friendship, hatred, or pity. The mind "perceives not truth easily when these "passions interfere *." This introduction is calculated with great propriety to make every person turn his eyes inward, and consider the state and impartiality of his mind. The orator then proceeds to enumerate particular examples of the miseries that had arisen from the defect of this temper; and in the end he applies the whole with masterly address to the affair of Cataline. The crimes of the conspirators by this conduct are artfully veiled; the best side of the object is only exposed to the eye of the spectator; and those very passions are at last powerfully stimulated in a bad cause, whose influence at first was so professedly disclaimed.

2. Elegance of sentiment as it thus requires in some instances what is unpleasing to be shaded, and what has either real

---

* " Omnes homines P. C. qui de rebus dubiis consultant ab odio, amicitia, ira, atque misericordia vacuus esse debet. Haud facile animus verum providet ubi illa officiunt." Conjurat. Catal.

or apparent beauty to be shown in all its attractions, so in others we observe and acknowledge it more obviously to predominate, when in close argumentation an adversary is confuted without having reason to feel that mortification which ariseth from this circumstance; and whose vanity is rendered subservient to his instruction, by being gratified at the time that his reasoning is disproved. Of this address no man ever was a greater master than Socrates, who puts it in practice succeffively upon every occasion when he is engaged with men who could not otherwise be drawn into conversation.—When Euthyphron acquaints him, that he had come to the Areogapus to prosecute his father for murder, and attempts to justify his conduct by telling some childish stories of Jupiter's conduct to Saturn; Socrates, instead of laughing at his folly, applies himself to his ruling passion, and refutes his principles, while he appears willing to adopt those as his own. After having founded the depth of his antagonist, and brought him to acknowledge that he believed

lieved the Gods to differ often from each other in opinion, he thrusts a vein of refined irony into his discourse, and raiseth scruples in the mind of Euthyphron, upon his own principles with regard to the justice of his cause, happily calculated to make him desist from the prosecution.—
" Excellent Euthyphron (says he), since you
" say that the gods form different judg-
" ments of right and wrong, truth and
" falshood, and act according to these
" judgments, you have not yet explained
" to me the nature of holiness; for I did
" not ask you what is at the same time
" sacred and prophane, pleasing to one
" god, and disagreeable to another:— so
" that it would not be wonderful if you,
" by getting your father punished, should
" do an action agreeable to Jupiter, but dis-
" agreeable to Cœlus and Saturn; pleasing
" to Vulcan, but offensive to Juno; and
" judged of differently by the other deities
" according to the character of each *."

3. In

---

* Ουκ αρα ο προμην απεκρινω, ω Θυμασιε. ε γαρ τετο γε πρωτων, ο τυγχανει ταυτον ον οσιον τε και ανοσιον·

3. In many instances likewise, a peculiar degree of elegance is discovered in turning a thought (principally of the panygirical kind) so happily as may surprise the reader into immediate approbation. This happens, most commonly, when there is an artful disposition of circumstances concurring to throw light on some object, at once agreeable and unexpected. Of the kind here mentioned, is the following noble complement to Cato, in which the poet ineffably heightens his eulogium by a previous enumeration of grand and terrible circumstances.

    Jam nunc minaci murmure cornuum
    Perstringis aures: jam lituï strepunt;
    Jam fulgor armorum fugaces
    Terret equos, equitumque vultus.
    Audire magnos jam videor duces
    Non indecoro pulvere sordidos!——

ανοσιον· ο δ' αν Θεοφιλες η και Θεομισες ες-ιν, ως εοικεν· Ωςε ω Ευθυφρον ο συ νυν ποιεις τον πατερα κολαζων, ουδεν θαυμαςον ει τουτο δρων, τω μεν Διι προσφιλες ποιεις, τω δε Κρονω και τω Ουρανω εχθρον. Και τω μεν Ηφαιςω φιλον, τη δε Ηρα εχθρον. Και ειτις αλλος Θεων ετερος ετερω διαφερεται περι αυτου, και εκεινοις κατα ταυτα, &c. ΠΛΑΤΩΝ. Ευθυφ. τμημ. Θ.

Et *cuncta terrarum subacta*——
Præter *atrocem animum Catonis* * !

The concluding circumstance here, every reader will allow to have elegant beauty in its present connection. Even those, however, who are actuated by prejudice against the authors of Christianity, will, perhaps, acknowledge the apostle Paul's answer to king Agrippa to have merit (though not precisely of the same kind) in all respects equal to that of the courtly Roman in the preceding instance.—" Al-
" most (says the prince to him) thou per-
" suadest me to be a Christian." To which the apostle (standing in chains before his throne) replies: " I would to God that
" not only thou, but also all that hear me
" this day were both almost and alto-
" gether, such as I am,—*except these*
" *bonds.*" The last words here, as in the former example, are peculiarly striking. They give a polite air to the apostle's answer, and constitute what the ancients denominate urbanitas, and the versutum &

---

* Hor. Carmin. lib. iv. ode 1.

lepide

lepide dictum. Its effect upon Agrippa discovered the propriety with which it was applied to him; for he was prevented from setting his prisoner at liberty only because he had appealed to Cæsar.

4. The last method we shall mention here, of rendering sentiment elegant, consists in the artful introduction of a principal topic from circumstances whose connection with it, though close and particular, the mind does not perceive until it slides in as it were imperceptibly, and attracts attention by being carelessly represented. This appearance of the character treated of here, is rarely to be met with; and only in works of great ingenuity.—In Pope's excellent Preface to his miscellaneous writings, he proposeth to disclaim many performances that had been ascribed to him, as unworthy that honour, and to prevent, if possible, a repetition of this abuse. The manner in which he brings about his purpose is admirable.—" I be-
" lieve (says he, speaking of himself) no
" one qualification is so likely to make a
" good writer as the power of rejecting
" his

" his own thoughts, and it must be this
" (if any thing) that can give me a chance
" to be one. For what I have *published*
" I can only hope to be pardoned; but
" for what I have *burned*, I deserve to be
" praised. On *this account* the world is
" under some obligation to me, *and owes
" me the justice in return to look upon no
" verses as mine that are not inserted in
" this collection.*" Here the author's prin‑
cipal end falls, as it were, incidentally into
his discourse; no reader, without having
been previously acquainted with his purpose,
would expect it to be introduced here.
Yet the connection is natural, and we ap‑
prove at the same time of the writer's
judgment and address.

II. Difficult as it may appear from the
preceding observations, for an author to
be distinguished by elegance of sentiment,
yet even when this point is obtained,
something further is still requisite to con‑
stitute elegant Composition, if we include
under that phrase all that it ought to sug‑
gest. This something, so necessary to give
the last heightening to this character, is
undoubt‑

undoubtedly, an expreffion happily correfponding to thefe fentiments, and fetting off all to the higheft advantage. An eminent critic obferves of ftyle in general, " that of fuch importance is this fingle
" circumftance, as to have decided (in the
" art of poetry) the fuccefs of pieces de-
" fective in material points, and yet uni-
" verfally admired on this account only.
" He mentions as proofs of the truth of
" this remark, the Cid, and the Death of
" Pompey, both works of Corneille, but
" greatly defective both in character and
" œconomy. Thefe, he obferves, are yet
" preferred, contrary to the rules of the
" drama, to others diftinguifhed by fu-
" perior manners, and a plan regularly
" profecuted.—Why?—Becaufe the ftyle
" and the fentiment happily correfpond in
" the firft inftance:—in the laft, this af-
" finity is not to be difcovered. When
" the heart therefore is touched by the
" voice of nature, all the critical argu-
" ments in the world can never per-
" fuade a man to with-hold his appro-
" bation."

"bation *." This approbation every reader gives to a performance diſtinguiſhed by unaffected elegance of expreſſion, the natural effect of which is always to excite a very pleaſing ſenſation, even when we are inattentive to the cauſe.

Expreſſion, to whatever ſubject it may be applied, is ſaid to have elegance when certain natural graces are ſo happily diſpoſed in it, as to throw light on their objects without the glare of oſtentation; and when an eaſe, conſiſtent with dignity, is to be obſerved univerſally in the diſpoſition of words fitted to the various parts of a ſubject. It is difficult, if not impoſſible, in moſt caſes to give any clear and appropriated idea of this envied excellence, becauſe it is conſtituted by certain exquiſite ſtrokes, whoſe influence is felt by a reader of ſenſibility, though he cannot reſolve theſe into a regular ſyſtem, and account in a rational manner for the cauſe of his admiration. They are ſuch:

---

* See Du Bos' Reflex. Critique ſur la Poeſ. &c. tom. i. chap. 23.

Ut

Observations on Composition.

> Ut fibi quivis
> Speret idem, fudet multum, fruftraque laboret
> Aufus idem.   Hor.

Let us, however, try whether amidft fo many evanefcent beauties ready to diffolve like the fhade of Patroclus into air as foon as we attempt to lay hold of them, we cannot catch a few of the moft ftriking in their paffage, and hold thefe up as lights by whofe aid we may diftinguifh real from affected elegance of expreffion, in the various fpheres of Compofition.

In every juft imitation of any original, propriety requires that the peculiar and diftinguifhing graces, as well as the great outlines of any figure, fhould be tranfpofed faithfully into a copy. When we defcribe for inftance, a landfcape, it is obvious that we are pleafed in proportion as the rural fcenery is fo naturally difplayed as to prefent objects in their native and fimple decorations; as the *colours* of nature (if we may thus exprefs it) without being heightened are juftly delineated; and as certain ftriking features are fixed upon happily, and are fet off with graces which give

give beauty to the piece. Elegance in this imitation, requires that nothing in the description should be overwrought; that no foreign ornaments should be unnaturally forced in; that, in short, the words should imitate by a certain careless, but happy disposition, the easy negligence of nature in the various arrangement and attitudes of her objects.

     To the sylvan lodge
They came, that like Pomona's arbour smiled
With flowrets deck'd and fragrant smells;—but Eve,
Undeck'd, save with herself, more lovely fair
Than wood-nymph, or the fairest goddess feign'd,
Stood to entertain her heav'nly guest.——
    Raised of grassy turf
Their table was, and mossy seats had round
And on her ample square from side to side
All autumn piled, though spring and autumn here
Danced hand in hand.   MILTON.

Nature herself appears to have held the pencil in painting this group of beautiful figures, in which no false heightening or improper imagery is admitted; but the imagination of the poet, wandering at ease over the bowers of Eden, adorns its descriptions with objects so animated as to dissipate

dissipate the languor arising from insipid uniformity, while propriety takes place in the disposition as well as choice of these which the mind contemplates with peculiar satisfaction. The whole is indeed perfectly simple, but it must be acknowledged to be elegant simplicity.

We are not, however, always to suppose that a representation of the external beauties of creation, in order to have the heightening of elegance, ought always to be enlivened either with figures that have real life, or even with an imitation of this circumstance by personification. A description may have great elegance in which the objects of still life (as they are called) appear in a certain natural arrangement, when recommended by no other character than harmonious and appropriated diction. In the following combination of pastoral beauties all is in the highest degree picturesque, though nothing is personified, and the structure of the period is such as to improve the effect of a most elegant assemblage.

> At secura quies, & nescia fallere vita
> Dives opum variarum ; at latis otia fundis,
> Speluncæ vivique lacus : at frigida tempe,
> Mugitusque boum, mollesque sub arbore somni
> Non absunt. VIR.

Expression acquires ineffable elegance upon some occasions from a vein of imagery happily blended with the sentiment, and coalescing with it in such a manner as that both must suffer by the slightest transposition. Such is the character of Sappho, drawn by Horace:

> *Spirat* adhuc Amor,
> Viventque commissi calores
> Æoliæ fidibus puellæ. Ode ix. lib. 4.

The image wrought here so exquisitely into the character, reminds us of the delicate shading in the most masterly drawings, which seems to die away insensibly into air, or fades by imperceptible degrees into the ground-colour of the piece. By attempting to disjoin these, we encroach upon something which we meant to have preserved, and are sensible that the piece must be disfigured by the most minute alteration.

In our remarks on elegant Compofition, we have endeavoured to fhow in what cafes this characteriftic excellence diftinguifheth the fentiment of a performance; and we have pointed out examples in which it is confpicuous in the thought and expreffion of a work mutually reflecting light on each other. In fome inftances however, thoughts that have no peculiar merit of themfelves, and which in an ordinary drefs would have been wholly overlooked, become fignificant by being expreffed with a certain natural eafe which gives an air of unaffected elegance to the whole. In this branch of the character here treated, we muft allow Anacreon to be wholly peculiar and inimitable. When this writer tells us, that " he cares not for " Gyges the king of the Sardians; that " gold has no attractions for him; that " he envies not tyrants; and that his de- " fire is to pour unguents on his body, " to crown himfelf with rofes, and let to- " morrow provide for itfelf;"—fuch circumftances in a tranflation may appear foreign and impertinent. Yet in the original

ginal that " curiosa felicitas dicendi," that happy choice and disposition of words, which it is a vain attempt to imitate, confers graces on these slight remarks which render them the objects of elegant entertainment *.

In

---

* Ου μοι μελει Γυγαο,
Του Σαρδεων ανακτος·
Ουθ' αιρεει με χρυσος,
Ουδε φθονω Τυραννοις.
Εμοι μελει μυροισι
Κατα βρεχειν υπηνην.
Εμοι μελει ροδοισι
Καταςεφειν καρηνα.
Ου Σημερον μελει μοι, &c. ANAK. εις Εαυτ.

The character of this bard the reader will find drawn more particularly, and the elegance of his composition exemplified, in the Essay on Lyric Poetry, p. 55, &c.— The ingenious Abbé du Bos has preserved a beautiful ode in his Reflections on Poetry and Painting, in which a thought, as simple as any of the preceding, is rendered striking by the graces of elegant expression. It is a piece of the Abbot Chaulieu, whose purport is only this, that he would die in the place where he was born. We admire, however, the colour with which it is ornamented.——

Fontenay lieux delicieux
  Ou je vis d'abord la lumiere,
Bientot au tout de ma carriere
  Chez toi je joindrai mes ayeux.

Muses,

In the sphere of Composition, as no excellence whatever is more universally envied and admired than that of elegance, so there is none in every sense more difficult to be acquired. This is obvious, from the bad success of many attempts that have been made to imitate writings distinguished by this character. Among the imitators of the manner of Anacreon, few have ever been able to catch the spirit, and transfuse the graces of this original*. Plato in the same manner stands unrivalled among Greek philosophers, and Horace and Petronius among the Romans †. A

man

Muses, qui dans ce lieu champetre
   Avec soin me f'ites nourir,
Beaux arbres qui m'avez vu naitre,
   Bientot vous me verrez mourir.—
               Du Bos. c. xxxiii. v. 1.

* Prior, among our own writers, seems to have approached nearest to this original. Some of his pieces are happily Anacreontic. Fontaine is an inimitable original himself.

† These authors (the last particularly) are selected here, because elegance is their principal characteristic. Cicero has this in common with many other excellencies, but upon the whole, the " teres atque rotundus " (as Horace calls it) characteriseth his copious

expression

man must have received from nature a power of perceiving certain exquisite connections, in order to be denominated elegant in the sense assigned here to that epithet, and a facility of selecting and of applying those graces to description or sentiment, that are just the most suitable and becoming. We must make a distinction however betwixt these powers, the one of which regards perception, and the other execution. Though neither are conferred universally, yet many persons are enabled by the former to observe and to feel the effect arising from an assemblage of objects elegantly decorated, who yet would fail in an attempt to form so beautiful a combination; because with sensibility to relish these beauties when presented to the mind, its powers may be inadequate to the task of creating them. That energy of thought by which the

---

expression more remarkably than any other signature, and in studying a model of elegance it is proper to have that presented to us which offers principally to our view the various forms of this distinguishing quality.

most

most appropriated colouring is immediately applied to ideas, and the most suitable expression is selected with ease to render these universally agreeable, is wholly distinct from the power by which we judge of a just or inadequate combination; the last of which extends no further than to enable the person possessed of it to avoid gross defects in Composition, and to be characterised upon the whole by negative description.

To deny (whatever truths may be in these observations) that an elegant taste may be improved, if not created, and its influence rendered conspicuous in execution as well as theory, by the study of unexceptionable models, would be as absurd as to deny that the dignity of a good mien may be heightened by having frequented the best company; or that the expression of an amiable countenance becomes more attractive by a happy and graceful disposition of suitable ornaments. Though, therefore, we cannot suppose in the present case, that he whose natural powers are deficient, will by any process of obfervation be enabled to execute with maftery, and to throw out thofe graces that give elegance to Compofition; yet, by having attended to the effect of thefe in the writings of others, he may avoid the oppofite extreme in his own; and in the conduct of philofophical deduction, while the arguments may carry conviction to the underftanding, the ftyle of an author's compofition will thus be often entertaining, and at no time vulgar or difgufting.

It ought always to be obferved, that an *expreffion* unexceptionably accurate, if not really elegant, may be obtained by imitation and attention much more eafily than the means by which *fentiments* acquire this character. The art of turning a period with harmony may be learned with more facility than that of expofing a thought in the happieft point of view, or of rendering a feries of fentiments agreeable by a certain juft and beautiful difpofition, becaufe the firft of thefe depends principally upon an harmonious ear; whereas the laft requires tafte, difcernment, and fenfibility.

As to elegance likewise, considered simply with regard to expression, we must distinguish that kind of it which ariseth from a certain pleasing arrangement of words, from that which is observed in the invention, beauty, and disposition of images, improving every object by an appropriated colour, and adding to a piece the last exquisite shading that renders it complete. The attainment of the first of these purposes depends in a great measure upon the choice of proper models for imitation; principally upon having made a just selection in very early life. There is (as the study of works composed at ages remote from each other will convince any man) a certain mode of expression, by which contemporary writers in one (even classical) age may be distinguished as obviously from those who at a considerable distance have either preceded or come after them, as that by which two flourishing at the same time are known and discriminated. The difference indeed becomes more strikingly conspicuous, when we compare a polite with a barbarous age,

than when we judge from any intermediate periods *; becaufe this prefents
to us fuch a profpect as the fame face feen
in youth and in old age. Time, which
at a middle period would have been obferved to alter without impairing its ex-

---

* Longinus, who lived in the reign of Aurelian
and Zenobia, compared with the beft writers of the
age of Auguftus, is indeed a remarkable exception to
the rule here laid down; but not only are we to confider this as an inftance almoft wholly fingular, but
we may afcribe it either to that native fublimity of
imagination, which (as we fhall fhow afterwards) is
the character of all others leaft apt to be impaired by
any external circumftances; or to an happy felection
of models in the firft ftage of life, which Longinus
might have been prompted to make by his own exquifite difcernment. Both thefe caufes probably con-
curred to prevent this eminent critic from being
tainted by the tafte of an age confiderably degenerated.
The firft mentioned is evidently confpicuous in the
grandeur of his own fentiments, and in that keen fenfibility with which he appears to have entered into
thofe of others:—the laft is obvious from the autho-
rities quoted by him from the beft ftandards handed
down by antiquity. A writer converfant wholly with
thefe, and fitted at the fame time by nature to form
great conceptions, we might have pronounced fecure
againft the contagion of falfe tafte, and qualified to
tranfpofe by imitation thofe excellencies into his work,
whofe beauty he at the fame time felt and developed.
Milton is an example of this kind.

preffion,

pression, will be seen in this last stage to have made a remarkable change upon the whole: but the steps that have led to this are real though imperceptible, and at any confiderable interval their effect would have been obvious.

We must, after all, confider it at first view as fomewhat extraordinary that men, living at a period however remote, who might have imitated the perfect models of the Auguftan age handed down as patterns, fhould yet have adopted the barbarous and unintelligible jargon of their own. But this conduct ought principally to be af-cribed to the first bias imprinted on the mind, and to the writings with which it was converfant. An individual, how ingenious foever, and diftinguifhed by nature with elegant tafte, yet forming himfelf at first upon models lefs perfect than thefe already mentioned, or carried away by the prevailing character of his age and country, gradually falls into a manner which thefe circumftances contribute fo neceffarily to finifh, different perhaps from that which

which nature, unwarped by fashion and prejudice, would have taught him to assume. Elegant Composition, considered as perfected by the union of easy language, and of images disposed with grace and propriety, cannot be obtained when the mind is straitened in any exertion; and is impaired indispensably by the accidents here enumerated. In order therefore, as much as possible, to prevent their effects, the works that are first perused by a man of genius at any time whatever, ought to be such as are universally acknowledged to be characterised principally by the graces that constitute elegance. A *sublime* imagination will preserve its original bias, and will throw out strong examples of it, in whatever age the man possessed of this faculty may live, and by whatever circumstances (a total want of education excepted) its influence may be counteracted. This is one of those vivid and indelible characters so forcibly stamped upon the mind, as to resist the power of causes by which weaker ones are eradicated.

dicated *. The same remark may be made of this faculty when principally characterised

---

* Of the truth of this observation, the celebrated Ossian affords a distinguished example among our own countrymen, as Dante, Camoens, and Ariosto, (though flourishing indeed at later periods) exhibit among foreigners.. The spirit of Lada, and ghosts of the Calledonian bard; the machinery introduced by Dante in order to give poignancy to his exquisite satire; the Adamastor of the Portuguese, introduced with such grand and noble circumstances; and the various imagery thrown out with great sublimity of imagination, though without much regularity by the Italian;—these furnish incontestible proofs that this great character of Composition is to be met with universally in the works of distinguished geniuses, in whatever age they may happen to live. It is true that Ariosto lived in the sixteenth century, at the time of the resurrection of letters: but as learning was then only beginning to emerge from the night of Gothic ignorance, neither his work, nor that of Camoens is distinguished by the graces of elegant Composition as a characteristical excellence. Examples of sublime, and of pathetic description are to be met with universally in the writings of both. Ossian, in the same manner distinguished by grandeur, luxury, and exuberance of imagination, was conversant with no objects, and beheld no manners from which he might be enabled to obtain the graces that constitute elegance. The language in which he wrote, (musical as it is said to be), must have been unequal to the expression of elegant sentiment, (such as we have had occasion to exemplify) and some strokes of

terised by strength and energy. These last are so far from requiring a classical age to call them out into action, that we observe them often most conspicuously predominant in times of darkness and barbarism. It is otherwise with the character of elegance, which marks upon all occasions the productions of improved society, and is never the capital ingredient of a performance either composed by an illiterate author, or the work of a rude and barbarous age *. In order, therefore, to acquire

---

of description, finished with great delicacy, scattered through his writings, and through the writings of others in similar circumstances, are like flowers rising in a wilderness, whose beauty might have been highly improved by a cultivated soil, an happy exposure, and a favourable sun.

* In the savage state we may expect to meet with strength and vigour of thought, as well as of expression, particularly in the detail of transactions, because the rougher passions are in such a state taught to exert themselves with a certain desperate ferocity, whose influence appears in Composition. Accordingly, in the works of the *bards* of these times (the criteria by which we can best judge of the taste and manners of an age) strength of expression, and of colouring, is a signature more universally to be discerned, than in the more finished productions of our own. The ingenious

acquire this character, or at least to improve as highly as possible the propensity of nature, a man of genius, after having gained a just and appropriated idea of elegance, as relating both to expression and sentiment, should endeavour, by having attended particularly to every appearance of this excellence, and by attempts to imitate it in whatever manner it is apprehended, to carry his general observations into practice, and transfuse a portion of that spirit into his own Composition, whose influence he hath marked so justly in that of others.

---

nious Dr. Blair has illustrated this remark in his Dissertion on the Poems of Ossian, by translating a Gothic poem preserved by Olaus Wormius, in his work De Literatura Runica. " This (says our critic, after " having presented us with the work) is such poetry " as we might expect from a barbarous nation.—It " breathes a most ferocious spirit. It is wild, harsh, " and irregular; but at the same time *animated and* " *strong*; the style in the original highly figured and " metaphorical." Blair's Dissertat. quar. edit. p. 11. The same nervous expression distinguisheth the performances of Chaucer among our own countrymen; and for the reason already adduced, will generally be most conspicuous in the productions of a barbarous age.

Let

Let it be observed, that we desire as little in the present, as in any other case, a man of genius to bind himself down to a servile imitation of any model, however beautiful. Amidst all the objects that art or experience can assemble to promote intellectual culture, the *original expression* of the mind, like the original stamina of the body, remains unalterable, though this expression will be set off by these to the highest advantage, when neither impaired by timidity, nor distorted by affectation. An herb withering in the shade, and expanding its leaves, or exhaling fragrance in the sun, presents an image corresponding to the present subject. In both situations a discerning eye will trace the same lineaments, however different their external appearance. But in one case the foliage is shrunk and contracted;—in the other its colours are heightened, its foliage opened, and its beauty greatly improved by exposure and cultivation.

As a principal means to assist us in the art of rendering Composition truly elegant, we must endeavour to guard against errors that

that carry the appearance of this character so plausibly as not to be easily known from reality. Thus an attempt to introduce *brilliance* into Composition by a certain quaintness of epithet, and artful disposition of pretty images substituted with no propriety or significance, passeth upon many readers for elegance, though really incompatible with it at the bottom. An imagination always looking out for metaphors, and applying these without proper direction or discernment, is usually the cause of this false delicacy. When Ovid makes Laodamia say to Protesilaus, who was engaged in the Trojan war,

> Timeo: quotiesque subit miserabile bellum.
> More nivis lachrymæ sole madentis eunt.
> Oft as the wars tremenduous scenes appear,
> Like snow dissolving, drops th' unceasing tear.

The strained allusion employed here, has some appearance of elegance at first view, but taste rejects it as a prettiness indicating at least want of attention, if not a defect of discernment.

We ought likewise to distinguish elegance, properly so called, from purity or chastity of language; the latter of which regards

regards the conftruction and propriety of words, while the former relates to the graceful and harmonious ftructure of periods. By the harmony of periods is not meant a long ftring of words rounded in an elaborate and uniform manner. This end is obtained by a natural and judicious variety, adapted properly to the different branches of a fubject, and to that particular kind of fentiment into which an author may happen to fall. It would be an eafy matter to enlarge this part of our work, by examples of falfe delicacy in the ftyle of Compofition; but as we have already confidered in what manner elegance may be difcovered, either in the fentiment or expreffion of a performance, and have attempted to confirm, by fuitable illuftrations, our remarks on the means that conftitute this character, a further enlargement on the defects of writers, otherwife eminent, would be at the fame time difagreeable and unneceffary.

We fhall therefore difmifs this fubject when we have juft obferved in general, that however certain authors, from a confcioufnefs sciousness perhaps of their own inability to obtain the graces that constitute elegance in the art here treated of, may affect to despise it, yet it is by these that the human heart is most powerfully captivated, and consequently the end of instruction most effectually accomplished. By a conduct of this kind, a man discovers his own want of understanding, which would suggest to him that a man, in whatever point of view it may appear to himself, acquires significance in proportion as the purposes are important to which it may be rendered subservient. The politeness and fluency of Petronius, and the simple elegance of Anacreon, make vices and trifles the sources of entertainment, while a writer who possessed a vein of sterling wit, but without the power of setting it off with this character of Composition, is censured with reason, and is perused with disgust.

—— Nostri proavi *Plautinos* & numeros, et
Laudavere sales, nimium patienter utrumque,
Ne dicam stulte mirati ; si modo ego & vos
Scimus inurbanum lepido seponere dicto,
Legitimumque sonum digitis callemus & aure.

SECTION V.
Of sublime Composition.

THE characters of just Composition, whose nature and use we have attempted to explain in the preceding sections, belong (as we have seen) indiscriminately to every branch of the art without exception; and the execution of any performance must be judged deficient in which these are not united. Simplicity, perspicuity, and elegance, we are therefore to consider as criteria at the same time universal and indispensable, in which respects they differ from the ingredient of sublimity, whose influence extends principally to certain known species, and when exerted in others is a noble but unexpected decoration, whose presence excites high approbation, though its absence might have been marked without censure. There is likewise another circumstance peculiar to the grand in Composition, considered as a character of the art by which it is distinguished from those that have formerly

formerly been enumerated. It is, that while these may characterise the *expression* of a performance when there is nothing striking or uncommon in the *sentiment*; and though on that account we may examine separately the thought or description, and the language that conveys it, yet in the article of sublimity these must always be contemplated together, and in order to constitute this excellence, there must be an invariable co-operation of both. A work in which, upon the whole, there is nothing either new or extraordinary, when the thoughts are examined apart, may yet be distinguished by simplicity, perspicuity, and even elegance of diction:—but an exalted idea naturally swells out the language to adequate emphasis*; and when

---

* Longinus, in his enumeration of the sources from which sublimity is derived, considers expression " as a kind of common stratum, or foundation for " this magnificent superstructure, which however " may be deficient so as to render the whole of no " effect." Περι Υψ. τμημ. H. But this assertion upon strict examination, will not perhaps appear to have been closely investigated. For it is here supposed

when the latter (however founding) is unsupported by majesty of sentiment, we denominate it timid and bombast.

The

---

posed, that to a mind possessing all the sources of sublimity, a power may be denied of clothing its ideas in significant language. Προυποκειμενης ωσπερ εδαφυς τινος κοινυ ταις πεντε ταυταις ιδεαις της εν τω λεγειν δυναμεως, ης ολως χωρις κδεν. Ubi sup. But this is a case rarely, if ever, to be met with. An imagination filled with a great idea, will adopt an expression as naturally appropriated to the object, as a man stimulated by the impulse of any passion finds words expressive of his feeling. In the first instance the mind may labour with the greatness of some vast conception, and may find it difficult to select words proportioned to its sublimity; but still the thought will give strong significance to such as are fixed upon, which, whether adapted or not with perfect propriety, will receive elevation from the sentiment. It is not, therefore, true, that when an idea truly sublime is formed, and distinctly comprehended by the mind, expression can be defective, so as to render it of no effect. But admitting that a person, capable of thinking in this manner, should be able to make use of no words but such as are mean and wholly disproportioned, it is obvious, that notwithstanding this inconvenience by which an alteration would be made on the external appearance of an object, its intrinsic value would continue to be the same; and though sublimity is imperfect when there ceaseth to be a proportion betwixt the thought and expression; yet the former, far from being rendered

The province of the sublime in every kind of Composition is pre-occupied by a critic, whose noble work on this subject is so universally perused and admired by readers of the smallest classical knowledge, that an enlargement on this subject is in a great measure superseded by it. As a repetition, therefore, of the sentiments of Longinus would be useless on the present occasion, we shall endeavour (as every subject admits of being viewed in different lights) to avoid, as much as possible, an interference with this admired author, which could answer no important purpose either of entertainment or instruction. We

---

dered of no use by such an omission, would still produce an effect upon a mind able thoroughly to comprehend it, adequate to its excellence, and to the propriety of its disposition. But such an inequality when the mind is agitated by a ruling passion, and far more when imagination is filled with an exalted idea, we have no reason to expect. An object viewed indistinctly, cannot be clearly represented; but when it is at once magnificent and turned full to the faculty that surveys it, suitable words will occur as readily to delineate it with mastery, as the proper tools will be applied by a skilful artisan to give proportion, grace, and consistency to his work.

shall, therefore, separately consider by what circumstances sublimity is constituted in the various field of the extensive art here examined, and show in what manner the true may be distinguished from the false sublime:—the most proper method of improving upon the foundation laid by nature for the acquisition of this great quality will fall next to be examined, as necessary to render our view of it complete as a character of Composition.

I. The grand in this art, therefore, ariseth from the union of bold and elevated sentiments, with grace and dignity of expression. Of these, when traced to their original, imagination is in most cases the common parent. To the observations formerly made on the employments assigned to this power in the departments of science, it is here only necessary to add, that we ought to distinguish betwixt *one idea* greatly conceived, or *one circumstance* heightened by exquisite colouring; and thoughts united together in a comprehensive plan, which may be deemed *great* from the variety and complicated nature

of

of its materials. We never apply the epithet *sublime* to a production of this laft kind, whofe conduct is referred to the underftanding; and we denominate it *great*; in the fame fenfe as we would apply this phrafe to an empire confpicuous not for the grandeur of its palaces, but merely for the extent, and variety of its provincial territories. A comprehenfive fcheme, therefore, whofe parts are well adjufted, and obfervations that lay open the nature of a fubject, indicate the compafs and depth of an author's underftanding:—but one object truly noble, or even one mafterly ftroke in the delineation of a figure, difcovers a *sublime* imagination; and a congenial fpirit is never at a lofs, both to mark this character when it occurs, and to refer it when difcovered to its proper original.

We do not here mean by afcribing the fublime to the power of invention, either to contemplate this as acting independently of the reafoning faculty in the prefent office, or to reprefent fublimity as principally conftituted by the defcription of objects fubmitted to the cognifance of

fenfe.

sense. The range of fancy is immense; and whatever excites *admiration* falls within her province. A naked rock, a stupendous precipice, a ruined tower, and other external scenes of a similar kind, are presented in all the majesty of description by her pencil. But her influence extends no less to immaterial subjects, or rather these when coloured, impersonated, and presented vividly to the eye, form the highest and most conspicuous characters on which her creative energy is exerted. By the power therefore of imagination, innumerable themes, both in nature and art, are rendered subjects of admiration;— by the superintendence of reason, her flights are prevented from being extravagant.

There is, in description of all kinds whatever, a certain justness of colour (if we may thus express it), a certain relation betwixt the person or thing described, and the natural ideas formed of it by mankind in general, without which no object can be denominated sublime, or, indeed, be distinguished by any determinate character.

When

When Milton (the most sublime of poets) represents the Deity as " enthroned *above all height*;" when in the same spirit of exalted description *his skirts* appear " *dark with excessive bright*;" we are led to admire these daring and astonishing circumstances as the result of regulated, instead of censuring them as the ebullitions of extravagant imagination, by recollecting that both are mentioned of the *only Being* to whom they can be applied with propriety; the first filling the mind with the most exalted idea of his ineffable majesty; the last, by one of the happiest and most picturesque images ever seized by human imagination, representing the effulgence of splendor that surrounds him. Such circumstances as these, appropriated to any other object within the whole compass of nature, would be viewed as indications of an inventive faculty, great indeed, but uncontrouled in its operations, and unaided by that power which maintains consistency in every form delineated by the mind.

Here then we observe the provinces of the two superior faculties in producing sub-

sublime Composition placed in distinct points of view. As the former, therefore, conceives the original idea, so when this has been reviewed by the understanding with approbation, it suggests an expression adapted to convey it with suitable energy. Hence it happens, that though we often meet with flimsy thoughts clothed in pompous language, and rendered by this disproportion conspicuously ridiculous, yet we rarely, or never observe a thought, conceived with genuine sublimity, to be disfigured by mean and inexpressive epithets. The same intellectual power that rises to elevated sentiment, prescribes likewise an expression adequate to its majesty; as well as the colouring, or imagery, calculated to make the most vivid impression. Contemplated as the parent of the marvellous and admirable, the influence of imagination is by no means to be limited to the invention of what is grand in sentiment, or to the personification of what is inanimate in nature. These are, indeed, the themes that require her most strenuous exertion. But when we trace to this

power

power likewife, as to its original fource, the felection of well appropriated language, it ought to be remembered, that we afcribe no greater effect to it than the paffions, taken feparately, fhare with it in common; each of which dictates a diftinct expreffion, in proportion as it is gentle, or forcible; languid, or impetuous; by which, as an invariable criteria, we form an eftimate of the character or temper.

We muft not fuppofe, however, that this happy coalition of noble objects and fignificant diction, whofe concurrence is neceffary to give fublimity either to fentiment or defcription, can be perfectly obtained, even by the united effort of both intellectual powers, while unimproved by ftudy, experience, and practice. Art, in order to complete this character, muft improve upon the foundation of nature; and an author ought to be fo well acquainted with the manner of forming this combination in particular inftances, as that his own practice may be regulated by the theory he hath gained from experience. This circumftance it is, that renders the true

true sublime so uncommon, and so difficult an attainment. The irregular grandeur of a Gothic edifice, at the same time that it excites admiration, reminds us of an uncultivated age, and of a people yet unacquainted with the effects arising from a graceful assemblage of corresponding parts. There is a wildness here which pleaseth, as an imitation of nature in some of her rudest productions; but we behold with equal astonishment, and with higher approbation, a performance in this kind, finished by the exquisite strokes of an art concealed from our inspection, and wrought (though we perceive not the means) from models in which the union of grandeur and regularity forms the nearest approach to perfection.

II. These observations on the sublime in Composition, will be elucidated when we consider the various means by which this great character of the art is constituted. A little reflection will convince us, that sublimity ariseth from combinations, so diversified both of language and sentiment in the various spheres of Composition, as may

may indeed be discovered by taste, but cannot be reduced into a regular system. Some of these, however, it may here be proper to point out and exemplify, as well as to show in what manner the *true* may be distinguished from the *false* sublime, in order at the same time to direct a mind ambitious of acquiring this excellence, to the path that leads to it; and by detecting, from comparison, the errors of false representation to render these the objects of its avoidance.

A thought then sometimes becomes sublime, when the imagination seizing opposite circumstances, two subjects for instance, in the extremes of magnitude and littleness, of elevation and meanness, placeth the former in an exalted, and both in a picturesque point of view, by bringing these immediately into comparison. " I
" believe (says Socrates, in the celebrated
" dialogue formerly referred to) that this
" earth is an immense body; and to a su-
" perior Being (as he afterwards describes
" one) looking down upon it, we, who
" inhabit the countries that lie betwixt
" the

" the river Phasis, and the Pillars of Her-
" cules, appear scattered on the coasts of
" the Mediterranean like ants or frogs, as
" we behold them gathered in parcels
" about a lake*." There is something
noble in the idea exhibited here of the
world in general; and the contemptible
figure which many powerful nations make,
when compared with it, raises our conceptions of its extent and magnificence as a
work worthy of its Divine Architect. The
Being who looks on, likewise, we are disposed to admire as sublime and glorious,
in the same proportion as those whom he
contemplates are deemed to be little and
insignificant. A beauty of the same kind,
but incomparably more exalted, characteriseth the following passage in the work
of a celebrated modern poet, where the
Deity, by one stroke of his masterly pencil,

---

* Ετι τοινυν εφη, παμμεγα τι ειναι αυτο, και ημας
οικειν της μεχρις Ηρακλειων στηλων απο Φασιδος εν
σμικρω τινι μοριω ωσπερ περι τελμα μυρμηκας, η βατ
τραχους περι την θαλατταν οικουντας. Και αλλους αλ-
λοθι πολλους εν πολλοις τοιουτοις τοποις οικειν. ΦΑΙΔ.
τμημ. υη.

appears ineffably glorious from comparison with the moſt ſplendid of his works.

> O THOU whoſe *word* from ſolid darkneſs ſtruck
> That *ſpark* the SUN *.

This glorious orb of light, repreſented as a ſpark ſtruck out at once by the word of the Deity, placeth the Creator in a point of view inconceivably more ſublime than could have been attained by any detail, however animated, of his perfections. Viewed in oppoſition to the higheſt of his viſible works, which diſſolves before him into nothing, the mind is filled by this circumſtance with an idea as worthy of its original as it is poſſible for it to conceive.

As a great object is thus in general ſet off to the higheſt advantage by being placed in oppoſition to an inferior one, diſtinguiſhed by ſome real or ſuppoſed reſemblance, ſo in other caſes, when original, to be placed in a ſublime light is leſs dignified, and the imagination of the painter muſt ſupply its deficiencies by colour and

---

* Night Thoughts, p. 2.

expreffion; it is yet rendered exalted by a happy difpofition of fome preceding circumftances, without which we fhould have perceived in it nothing extraordinary.— Thus when Hector is going to part from Andromache, after many tender and natural expoftulations, the poet fays,

>Ως αρα φωνησας κορυθ' ειλετο φαιδιμος Εκτωρ
>Ιππουριν.
>
>Thus having faid, the glorious chief refumes
>His towering helmet, black with fhading plumes.
>
>POPE.

But what (it may be afked) is there great in this defcription of the Trojan heroe?— We muft look for this purpofe into the preceding interview, in which we fee this illuftrious prince taking a laft and melancholy farewel of his wife and child, in a fcene of mingled tendernefs and magnanimity; where, after having given a loofe to the fofter paffions, and appeared the tender father and affectionate hufband, he reaffumes the character of the hero, and, expreffing his ambition to be foremoft in defending his country, puts on his helmet, and goes, with unfhaken fortitude, to the battle.

This

This happy difpofition of circumftances as it gives dignity to an incident, otherwife inconfiderable in defcription, fo in narration it renders a character truely fublime; and fentiments, otherwife merely philofophical, the peculiar objects of admiration.—Socrates, reafoning againft the fear of death, and coolly running the comparifon betwixt what we enjoy in this life, and what we conceive of the next, appears merely in the light of an excellent philofopher. But Socrates, juft condemned to death himfelf, by a fentence flagrantly unjuft, entering calmly into the examination of this queftion before his judges *, without expreffing fear, anger, indignation, or refentment †; this great man

---

* After having faid that the friendly fpirit which prevented him from purfuing upon other occafions what was unfit, had given him no warning upon the prefent, he concludes, that this being looked upon his death as an happy event. This he proves by a philofophical inveftigation.

† Καὶ ἔγωγε τοῖς καταψηφισαμενοις μου καὶ τοῖς κατηγοροις οὐ πανυ χαλεπαινω. καιτοι οὐ ταυτη τη διανοια κατεψηφιζοντο μου καὶ κατηγορουν. ΑΠΟΛ. ΣΩΚ. τμημ. λγ.

endeavouring to prepare his accusers for meeting death with intrepidity when their own turn should come *, and requesting of them to punish his children after him, should these prefer opulence to virtue †, appears in a light almost divine. Every sentiment is ineffably dignified by the circumstances in which he is placed; the whole action is sublime in the highest degree, and the man appears exalted above the common level of humanity. It is a conduct of this kind upon which not only men, but even the gods themselves, were supposed to look down with admiration.

A description (particularly in the higher branches of poetry, where a series of actions are related) becomes wonderfully sublime by the introduction of a just and

---

* Αλλα και υμας χρη ω ανδρες δικαςαι ευελπιδας ειναι προς τον θανατον, και εν τε τουτο διανοεισθαι αληθες, οτι ουκ εςι ανδρι αγαθω κακον ουδεν, ουτε ζωντι, ουτε τελευτησαντι. Id. ibid.

† Τυς υιεις μου επειδαν εβησωσι, τιμωρησασθε ω ανδρες ταυτα ταυτα λυπουντας απερ εγω υμας ελυπων εαν υμιν δοκωσιν η χρηματων η αλλυ τυ προτερον επιμελεισθαι η αρετης. Ibid.

adequate.

adequate illuftration *. This method of obtaining fublimity is put in practice univerfally by all writers who dwell on great and magnificent objects. It is, however, as difficult to reach this fummit of excellence by the prefent, as by any means whatever, becaufe the image that conveys to us fuch an object ought to be equal at leaft, if not in fome refpects fuperior to its original. The underftanding of an author likewife, never appears more confpicuous in this high fphere of Compofition, than when it directs him upon fome occafions to avoid comparifon of what kind foever, as tending to depreciate, rather than exalt that to which no illuftration can be adequate †.

That

" On s' explique (fays a French critic with propriety on the fubject of illuftration) affez ordinairement, par des comparaifons & l'on s'en fert pour mieux faire concevoir ce que l'on propofe, & pour en donner une jufte idée. Elles ont deux qualitez effentielles; la premiere eft, que la chofe que l'on y employe foit plus connue, & plus aifee a concevoir que celle que l'on veut faire connoitre par fon moyen: & la feconde eft qu' il y ait un jufte rapport entre l'un & l'autre." Boffu du Poeme Epique, liv. vi. chap. 3.

† What another critic of the fame nation with the former, obferves of the poetic fable, may be applied
. here

That the image which is applied to set a great action or personage before our eyes ought to exceed, rather than fall below its original, will be acknowledged, if we reflect that the narration of any transaction, how animated soever, cannot affect us so strongly as if we had either been eye witnesses of, or personally interested in the event; and in order as much as possible to compensate for this deficiency, images are selected that impress a *vivid* idea of their original patterns upon the mind, and by exceeding the truth, excite in us nearly the same sensations with which we should have beheld it. By following out this train of observation, we may discover the origin of poetic licence (as it is called), and contemplate it in a much more rational and philosophical light

---

here with perfect propriety to its images. " La fable doit encore avoir deux qualitez pour estre parfaite: elle doit estre merveilleux, & elle doit estre vraisemblable. Elle devient digne d'admiration par la premiere, & elle devient digne de creance par la seconde. Quelque merveilleuse que soit la fable elle ne sera point d'effet si elle n'est vraisembable, &c." Rap. Reflex. sur la Poetique Oeuv. tom. ii. p. 103.

than

than is ufually done. That dignified perfonages, great actions, momentous revolutions, or aftonifhing events, might be difplayed for the purpofe of exciting a virtuous emulation, and of arrefting attention by ftrokes of mafterly eloquence, images are made ufe of whofe tendency principally is to exalt the imagination, or to awaken the paffions proper to be wrought on. While we are confcious of the end for which thefe are applied, reafon, in this cafe, overlooks a difproportion betwixt the image and the object to be illuftrated, which it would have cenfured in another as impertinent and injudicious: Thus it was foon obferved, that the end of poetic reprefentation could not be effectuated unlefs an indulgence was granted of the kind here mentioned. This indulgence therefore, has in all ages been permitted, and when the truth is not grofsly violated by circumftances abfurd and incredible, the mind confiders a certain difparity as adding to the beauty, and heightening the impreffion of the whole.

There is no perfonage of poetic ftory, either ancient or modern, defcribed with higher colouring, and in a greater variety of attitudes, than the *Satan* of Milton. Yet when he is compared by this fublime genius (in different parts of his work) to the fun in eclipfe *, to a comet †, to a planet ‡, and even to Atlas or Teneriff §, it is obvious, that thefe capital circumftances are mentioned rather as their fplendor, their portentous appearance, their magnitude, and their ftability, ferve to convey, in different points of view, fome idea of the attributes that are afcribed to him, than as thefe exhibit the exact proportions of his ftature, the real expreffion of his anger, or the unconquerable firmnefs of his ftrength and refolution. We admire the grandeur of that imagination which reprefents its object in fo many noble and picturefque attitudes, without either conceiving it to be fully equal to the comparifons in every circumftance, or

---

* Paradife Loft, b. i. l. 594.   † Id. b. ii. l. 708.
‡ Id. b. vi. l. 313.   § Id. b. iv. l. 987.

being

being offended becaufe we obferve fome inequality. The cafe is indeed different, when this inequality takes place in the illuftration as falling below the original. The end of poetic defcription (which is intended, as we formerly obferved, to fupply the emotions excited by perfonal infpection) is loft in this inftance; and a character intended to raife admiration, excites no other paffion than that of ridicule. It is (as we obferved formerly) a proof of an author's underftanding to avoid all comparifon, when the perfon or thing defcribed is either fuch as his imagination can illuftrate by no adequate image, or when it is fo great as that any illuftration muft neceffarily fall below it. There are, indeed, few things capable of being illuftrated, to which the genius of Milton was inferior. The *Deity himfelf*, only his judgment reprefented as fuperior to whatever falls within the compafs of human inveftigation. His ftrokes are therefore here as cautious and timid, as in other inftances thefe are daring and mafterly.

A very high degree of sublimity is often obtained by a sudden and abrupt interrogation *. An author may seize the imagina-

---

* This method of becoming sublime, acquires its excellence principally from exciting surprize, which an interrogation, or a series of these, may awaken, so as to make a very powerful impression. Here we must take care, however, not to include, under the denomination of sublimity, such strokes of eloquence as may have strength and pathos, though without that character of just elevation which constitutes this excellence. Without keeping this distinction in our eye, we shall be apt to confound with each other characters of Composition perfectly distinct; and what we do not thoroughly comprehend, we cannot hope successfully to imitate. Quintilian, distinguished as he usually is by exquisite taste as well as accurate discernment, seems somewhat inadvertently to have fallen into this mistake, by an example he produceth of sublimity from an oration of Cicero. Having made much the same distinction betwixt a comparison and translation, as figures of rhetoric, which we have found Aristotle making betwixt an image and a metaphor, b. I. sect. vi. p. 112. he proceeds to observe, that a wonderful degree of sublimity is often obtained by the translation as it is called, i. e. the giving life and action to an object wholly inanimate. The following bold interrogations, addressed to Tubero, he produceth as an example.—". Quid enim tuus ille Tubero deltrictus in acie Pharsalica gladius agebat? Cujus latus ille mucro petebat? Qui sensus erat armorum

imagination at once by employing this figure; and when his own mind is filled with the grandeur of some idea, may exalt in the same manner that of another, without entering into circumstantial detail. When the great POET, formerly mentioned, is going to paint the combat of Michael and Satan, as if at a loss to convey his idea with suitable strength, he exclaims,

> Who, though with the tongue
> Of angels, can relate, or to what things
> Liken on earth conspicuous, that may lift
> Human imagination to such height
> Of god-like power?— Book vi.

Without mentioning any particular circumstance here, relating to the combatants,

---

morum tuorum?" Cicer. pro Ligar. Quintil. lib. viii. cap. 6. The personification in this passage is undoubtedly strong and masterly in an eminent degree. But is it not an instance rather of the bold that animates, and of the *new* that surpriseth, than of the grand that swells and elevates the imagination? These are spheres that ought always to be considered as different; a point that can only be obtained by bringing to the standard of certain established rules, every example that falls under our cognisance, as we shall thus be able to refer every effect to its proper principle, and will be unembarrassed in our decisions.

the author leads us to form the higheſt notion of their mutual ability, and intereſts us ſtrongly in the event of a tranſaction upon which he enters with ſo much ſolemnity, and to the full deſcription of which he repreſents created intelligence as inadequate. It would be improper to multiply examples of ſublimity obtained by this figure, as after having the track pointed out, every reader of ſenſibility will ſuggeſt theſe for himſelf.

The laſt, and principal ſource of real grandeur in Compoſition, conſiſts of bold and animated perſonifications. By this figure a ſentiment is often placed in a light the moſt perfectly advantageous, as it becomes picturefque, and opens two inlets of pleaſure by gratifying at the ſame time the imagination and the ſenſes. It is on this account, that two of the moſt beautiful pieces of antiquity are ſo much, and ſo juſtly eſteemed; I mean the Hercules of Prodicus, and the noble portraiture of Cebes. We have, in a former work, conſidered this noble figure in a philoſophical light, and have endeavoured to account for its
various

various effects to which we here refer, as superseding an enlargement *. We need only at present to observe, that as the sublime in almost every case requires the picturesque to be united with it, and is perfected by this combination, the last mentioned character is never more completely obtained, than when impersonated figures are placed before the imagination with their proper insignia, and are represented as producing their natural effects. To the union of these circumstances in Composition, we shall find, upon recollection, that the most admired examples, both of ancient and modern genius, owe all their impression. Of this the winds in the Æneid rushing at the command of their sovereign to swell the agitated ocean †; the deities, in the Iliad, occupying every department of nature, and animating every action of the poem ‡; the angels, in the Paradise Lost, weilding the elements, and shaking the whole creation from its basis §,

---

* Essay on Lyric Poetry, let. ii. p. 101. octav. edit.
† Æneid. lib. i.   ‡ ΙΛΙΑΔ. pass.
§ Parad. Lost, book vi.

or (to mention perfonifications more perfectly allegorical) the figure of Melancholy, in Pope's Eloifa to Abelard *; of Night, in the Complaint of Young †; of the mountains ‡, the ocean, and the deluge §, in the Sacred writings, afford ftriking and remarkable examples. In each of thefe, taken feparately, and in many others of the fame kind, great objects, particular expreffions, and appropriated colouring, form a combination which we furvey with aftonifhment, and whofe effect upon a fufceptible mind is little inferior to that which would have arifen from beholding the originals.

The great art of rendering either figures imperfonated for exciting admiration, or even inanimate objects picturefque, lies in painting thefe with ftrokes that in order to be difcriminating muft be particular. It is the fame in eloquence, when an orator attempts to awaken the paffions. The fame expedient muft be ufed to penetrate

---

* Eloif. to Abel. v. 163, to 171.
† Night i. v. 18—25.
‡ Habak. ch. iii. v. 3.   § Pfalm. civ. v.

the

the heart in the laſt inſtance, which ſeizeth the imagination in the former. We may judge an object to be great from a deſcription which by no means renders it pictureſque, in the ſame manner as we may comprehend the general purport of obſervations, when we deſcend not to minute inveſtigation. Thus a mountain covering an immenſe track of country, or in general any object of uncommon magnitude, we acknowledge to be great in the common ſenſe of that word. But it is by the ſhadow trembling on the diſtant lake, by the cedar on its top ſeen like a ſhrub, and by the eagle hovering like a ſpeck above its ſummit: it is by theſe circumſtances that the whole becomes pictureſque; and the figure is more completely diſplayed by a ſingle ſtroke of this kind, than by any deſcription, however elaborate, of its ſize, height, and productions. When, on the other hand, the mind is to be powerfully impreſſed, and the heart to be penetrated by energetical repreſentation, this purpoſe is accompliſhed more effectually by one pointed appeal, by one ſtrong, ſignificant, and

and particular expreſſion, than by a general enumeration, though conducted with the utmoſt accuracy, of all the motives by which the heart of man ought to be touched, and his practice to be regulated. Such is the diſtinction which the mind always makes betwixt what is approved ſolely by the underſtanding, and what is felt by the heart.

It will here naturally be aſked, by what means has this particularly its effect?— The mathematician, who meaſures exactly the height and dimenſions of a mountain, and the poet who paints it, obtains each his purpoſe by being particular; as the philoſopher in the ſame manner who enumerates motives of conduct, deſcends from general to more minute diſquiſition, in order to impreſs more powerfully, the truth of certain propoſitions. But here lies the difference betwixt the faculty of reaſon operating by itſelf, and combined with imagination, ſo as to conſtitute diſcernment. In the one caſe the mind cannot, by the moſt elaborate reſearch, obtain that purpoſe, which in the other one maſterly terrly ftroke inftantly effectuates, without premeditation, ftudy, or induftry. It is the province of this laft power (as we have already feen *) to fuggeft immediately every circumftance that tends to place its object before the imagination in the moft ftriking point of view, and every motive that warms, agitates, and penetrates the heart. A great perfonage, therefore, reprefented as a principal actor in fome interefting tranfaction, moves at the fame time in a dignified fphere, and is rendered cognifable by the eye of the reader, in confequence of certain happy expreffions thrown into his countenance, an attitude juftly conceived, or an enterprize fuitably adapted; in which inftances the hand of a confummate artift is indicated from the choice of circumftances that carry fublimity to its utmoft height by uniting it with the picturefque and animated.

The grand, in the art here examined, confidered as it hath thus been with regard to its original, and to the various

---

* See book i. fect. 4.

combinations by which it is conftituted, in order to produce its proper effect, ought to be diftinguifhed from the bombaft or tumid, as it is called, which affumes upon many occafions fo nearly the appearance of genuine fublimity, as to impofe almoft equally upon the inexperienced, as upon thofe who are really defective in difcernment. We are as ready to miftake a feeming, for a real character of Compofition, as we are in life to give a man credit for certain virtues, who has fhadow without fubftance, and it is by experience only that we are undeceived of both. In order to prevent fuch a deception in the prefent cafe, let us enquire what is underftood by bombaft Compofition, and by what criteria it is to be known.

As we have feen that the true fublime demands an union of noble fentiments and elevated expreffion; the falfe it is obvious, muft argue a defect of either or both characteriftics. In general, we may obferve on this fubject, that though even a difcerning critic may be deceived by that appearance of this great character which

fo

so nearly resembles its reality; yet when he discovers upon recollection, that the pomp of language is elaborately displayed to set off either trite sentiments, or inadequate objects, he will conclude that the affectation of grandeur is then predominant, and that the turgid takes place of the genuine sublime. Expression, therefore, is said to be bombast when it is wrought up in a manner which the judicious reader perceives to be the effect of art rather than of nature; when much labour is bestowed to collect together sounding words and strong epithets, which pour upon the mind at once, and, like the noise of a torrent, are calculated rather to stun than to exalt it. Vulgar ideas conveyed in elaborate periods; images far fetched, discordant, or unappropriated *;

strained

---

* Καθαπερ ναυς μυρια διαδραμνσα κυματα, και πολλους εκφυγουσα χειμωνας (says Chrysostom, speaking of the Pharisee whose arrogance is condemned by our Saviour) ειτα εν αυτω τω σωματι τω λιμενος σκοπελω τινι προσαραξασα παντα τον εναποκειμενον απολλυσι θησαυρον. Ουτω δε και ο Φαρισαιος ουτος

strained epithets, and descriptions rendered shocking by unnatural circumstances *, expressed

ουτος τας πονας της νηςειας απομεινας, και της αλλης αρετης απασης, επειδη γλωττης ακ εκρατησεν εν αυτω τω λιμενι το φορτικον ναυαγιον υπεμεινε. ΧΡΥΣΟΣΘ. περι Φαρισ. This tumid and unappropriated image conveys to the mind of the reader no distinct idea of the action to which it is applied, and is besides wrought up with improper circumstances. In order to have rendered it properly adapted to the Pharaisee's situation, the ship ought to have been dashed on a rock, in consequence of the mariner's absurd confidence and precipitance. This man likewise, is not condemned for the offence of his tongue, but for the temper of mind that prompted to this transgression.

* In order to have a full idea of the fault mentioned in the text, let us observe in what manner three of the most celebrated ancients have described the same action. Homer says, that the horses who drew Hector's chariot, flew with great velocity from the left to the right wing of the battle.

Στειβοντες νεκυας τε και ασπιδας, αιματι δ' αξων
Νερθεν απας πεπαλακτο, και αντυγες αι περι διφρον
Ας αρ αφ' ιππειων οπλεων, ραθαμιγγες εβαλλον
Αι τ' απ' επισσωτρων.— ΙΛΙΑΔ. β.ς Λ.

This description is wrought up with strong and picturesque circumstances; but as the judgment of the poet prevented him from carrying it on to too great length, it presents only to the mind a general idea of the slaughter and desolation attending on battle. Virgil is still more cautious: when Æneas flies from
one

expressed likewise in language equally affected, are examples of that tumid diction which

---

one end of the battle to the other, to avenge the death of Pallas, he says only,

Proxima quæque metit gladio, latumque per agmen
Ardens limitem agit ferro.   Æneid. lib. x.

But Statius, describing his hero in the same point of view, lengthens out the detail very improperly in this place, and by attempting to be more circumstantial than the other, introduceth strokes which tumid epithets, and a false grandeur of diction, render equally shocking and unnatural.

    Hos jam ignorantes *teret* impius axis, at illi
    Vulnere femineces, (nec devitare facultas)
    Venturum super ora vident, jam lubrica tabo
    Fræna, nec infifti madidus dat temo, rotæque
    Sanguine difficiles, & tardior ungula fossis
    Visceribus: tunc ipse furens, in morte relicta
    Spicula, & e *mediis extantes ossibus, hastas*
    Avellit. Strident animæ, currumque sequuntur.
                                Thæbaid. lib. vii.

The feeling heart recoils from such a picture as this, and a regulated imagination rejects it with horror. There is, likewise, a certain decorum of character to which an author ought to attend in the expression of certain passions or actions. Circumstances that are natural and proper in some situations, are indelicate and shocking in others. A warrior in the height of his rage, upon being seized and reduced to servitude by an enemy, might call upon lions and tigers to tear him to pieces, rather than drag out life in inglorious bondage. But this language in the mouth of a lady,

which conftitutes the falfe fublime. Thefe are indications of an imagination vigorous but diftempered, and in a mind void of that fenfibility which reafon contributes to imprefs on a fufceptible heart, producing fuch effects as thefe faculties, when juftly combined, render objects of horror. It may be obferved here, that this propenfity to fwell out every circumftance by falfe colouring, and thus to exceed the proportions of nature will diftinguifh the man directed by it from another whofe mental powers are balanced with jufter equilibrium, as much when both are employed in placing the fame object before

---

in any cafe whatever, is ftrained and unnatural, as violating the foftnefs of the female character. When one of Ariofto's heroines fays, therefore,
——— quefto il lupo, il leon, l'orfo
Venga e la tigre e ogn' altra fera brava;
Di cui l'ugna mi ftracci e franga il morfo,
E morta mi ftrafcini a la fua cava.   Cant. x.
this difcourfe is extravagant, and this expreffion inflated, when we confider the perfon who pronounceth it. In other circumftances the fame ftrokes might have been highly interefting and pathetic. The reader will find many other examples of this kind in the Orlando, probably occafioned by the manners of an age not thoroughly refined.

the

the mind, as when their subjects are different. We have adduced an example of this in the preceding note. It is by comparing in this manner representations of the same kind at least, if not precisely of the same things, that we judge from the surest test, the effect produced by these, of their real value, or demerit; and when we have thus discovered the cause of a fault, unperceived formerly, in the performance of another, the same discernment leads us to correct it in our own.

Should it be necessary to lay down any other rule for avoiding the tumid in Composition (which to a man of true discernment, is more disgusting than any other blemish in the art, as indicating more conspicuously a defective understanding) we would advise a young writer to avoid, as much as possible, the perusal of *declamatory* works, which are very inadequate models, and yet are imitated by a man of genius with so much facility, as renders the trial agreeable. By falling into this manner, he will gradually learn to substitute *words* in the place of *things*; and having his ear filled with a founding period, will overlook the superficial sentiment often conveyed in it. The exterior attractions of the style of Composition, are like feathers beautifully variegated with an assemblage of colours floating on the surface of a stream impregnated with gold. With no other recommendation than a beautiful outside, they arrest the eye of a young and uninformed spectator. He may please himself with placing these in certain striking arrangements, and may thus discover that they have their use. But it is by searching the stream to the bottom, that he will be taught not to reject the original objects of his choice as wholly contemptible, but to consider their comparative utility, and value them proportionally.

We do not, however, mean when we thus advise a man of genius to avoid such branches of Composition in very early life as may render his own expression inflated and turgid, to recommend the same cautious procedure when his taste is properly formed, and when he is able to
distin-

distinguish appearance from reality so justly as not to be imposed upon by the former. In this situation he will receive information from observing the faults, even of performances excellent upon the whole, as he will at the same time judge of the cause from which these are derived, and of the method most happily adapted to correct them. With regard to the present subject more particularly, we may affirm with truth, that the same vigour of imagination which directed improperly, produceth tumid Composition, justly regulated, would have rendered it sublime. The first of these, indeed, is commonly supposed to accompany either objects or sentiments themselves superficial, or at least superficially examined. But it is certain, that the phrase tumid or bombast, applied to any branch whatever of the art, indicates a certain disproportion betwixt the thing represented, and the words employed for this purpose, and takes place, even when the idea is really great and important, as often as the diction by being studiously heightened with swelling epithets, is deemed to exceed that natural simplicity which excludes superfluity.

It is univerfally acknowledged, that the genuine sublime is no where to be met with in higher perfection, than in the Paradise Lost. The ingenious author of the Life of Milton, imputes, and no doubt with truth, some part of that amazing grandeur which the imagination of this poet obtained, to his having indulged himself early in reading romances.*. But " along with the honey sucked from these weeds," some parts of their noxious quality would appear, likewise, to have tainted the Composition, even of this great genius. Hence some critics have censured his expression as inflated, even when the most sublime ideas are conveyed in it. In early life, therefore, what may have made some impression upon such a mind as that of this distinguished poet, we may naturally judge to have an effect much more conspicuous upon a genius of inferior order, susceptible of the same effect from

---

* See Fenton's Life of Milton.

models

models improperly selected, and less able to detect their faults, or to resist their influence. A perusal, which, upon the whole, was beneficial in one case, in another will produce the bad, without the good effect; and taste will be vitiated instead of being justly directed by the false model of imitation that is placed before the mind.

Upon the whole, the utmost purpose that culture, however conducted, can reach in directing to the attainment of sublimity appears to be, that a man of moderate genius may be taught to distinguish with great propriety, the sublime of sentiment, or of description, from that swelling diction in which neither upon examination is conspicuous. He may feel very powerfully, the effect arising from that assemblage of circumstances which gives grandeur to Composition, and when he cannot accomplish a complete, will be deterred from attempting a partial imitation. The inventive power likewise, by the steady contemplation of objects calculated to call it out into exercise, may acquire an energy,

and even compass superior to that which
nature, unimproved in this manner, would
have enabled it to obtain. These acqui-
sitions, valuable in themselves, are enhanced
greatly by the additional knowledge which
a man of discernment gains by such observation of the real strength and proper
sphere of his faculties. False ideas of an
excellence, or a partial representation of
it, engage a man at best in a fruitless pursuit, which, when followed out to the
utmost, produce in him only regret for
not having thoroughly comprehended his
work before he engaged in it. He, therefore, whose imagination is capable of
making no extraordinary exertion, by acquiring a just idea of what is truly sublime, will learn upon trial to imitate only
such beauties as fall within his sphere;
while that person, on the other hand, who
may have been fitted by nature to join
great conceptions with adequate execution
will find by being accustomed early to
contemplate what is truly admirable, the
path to this excellence at last laid open to
him. Instead, therefore, of studying the
decoration

decoration of language as a principal ingredient of it (a miſtake of which a young mind is naturally ſuſceptible) he will diſcover this laſt to be wholly of ſecondary conſequence, as always accompanying elevated ſentiment, and though often obtaining where this great characteriſtic is not to be met with, yet never deficient where it is.

SECTION VI.

Of Nervous Compoſition.

THERE appears, at firſt view, to be a very cloſe affinity betwixt ſublime, and nervous, or forcible Compoſition, by which laſt term we underſtand ſtrength and energy, either of thought, of expreſſion, or of both taken together. Theſe, however, take their riſe from very diſtinct exertions of the intellectual powers, and produce very different effects. Sublime Compoſition is principally known by that height to which it exalts imagination; the forcible

forcible or strenuous, on the contrary, by the strength and duration of that impression which it makes either upon this power, or upon that of understanding. The one conversant always with the grand and magnificent, demands high colouring and copious illustration;—the other is commonly most perfect in its kind when the fewest words are employed, and is always weakened by diffusion. A man of sublime genius, describing the sun as an object incomparably glorious, would dwell upon the extent and splendor of the orbs enlightened by him: whereas an idea of his influence would be *forcibly* conveyed by representing the penetrating power of his rays in some particular instance. In short, a man may have strength of intellect who possesseth not sublimity of imagination, though he who has completely obtained the last quality hath always a power of exercising the former. The sublime analised into its principles, consists of great ideas strongly conceived and vividly painted; but a mind whose range is less comprehensive, may carry conviction

viction to the judgment by strenuous representation, or strike remorse to the recoiling heart by a particular and forcible appeal.

This masterly character of Composition is always the indication of exquisite sensibility, and most commonly the result of it. This observation admits of easy proof. The impression made by any representation upon the mind of a reader, must undoubtedly bear a proportion to that which the original objects imprinted upon the thought of the author. We have here said, that the one of these must *bear a proportion* to the other, it must not be concluded that this proportion will be perfect. Ideas, even when expressed with the greatest energy, lose always a part of their effect by being conveyed even in words that may be deemed most significant. The mind takes into its first draught certain objects, or particular strokes, which it cannot delineate with adequate emphasis (in whatever sphere likewise we suppose it to be employed)
whose

whose absence necessarily weakens the impression, and the effect of the whole. In proof of this remark, we may refer every man who has made a trial of this kind to the testimony of experience; and those whose powers are capable of making the most vigorous exertion, will probably be most sensible of its truth. A mind, therefore, whose feelings are weak, or whose powers though able to survey objects accurately is but slightly impressed by them, may be rational or methodical, but can never be interesting; and the secondary impression (as it may be called) still falling short of the original, its work will cease at last to excite attention.

We shall here consider that energy of mind which gives rise to this striking signature of just Composition, as exerting its influence on the sentiment, the diction, and illustrations or images, employed in the various branches of the art. After having viewed it in these lights, we shall endeavour to account for the inequality that takes place in many instances in the works

works of the same author, characterised at one time by vigorous execution, as at others by languor, and imbecility. This will lead us to make some general remarks on the causes that deprive language of its due force in particular cases, and on the method most proper to be used for avoiding, or for correcting this weakness.

I. A thought, in any field of speculation whatever, is said to be strongly conceived when its significance is such as to command attention, and to impress very powerfully that faculty to which it is principally addressed. Sometimes, without having perused a work, we may apply this epithet with propriety to the mind that conducts hypotheses or theory only upon hearing this last represented, when we discover in it not novelty only, which of itself excites no other sensation than that of surprise, but a certain strenuous, and daring exertion of intellect, that indicates energy and vigour. When we hear, for instance, of a philosopher who undertakes to disprove the existence of matter, the novelty
of

of the subject strikes us with surprize, and we even expect ingenious disquisition in the prosecution of it. Refined investigation, metaphysical distinction, and every indication of subtle genius, we suppose will be displayed in such a field; and upon meeting with these our expectations are gratified. But how different are the ideas excited upon hearing represented the plan of Burnet's Theory of the Earth!—The shell of the globe burst open at the deluge by the waters lodged within its cavity as in an immense reservoir; the rocks, mountains, precipices, promontories, islands formed in different parts by this universal rupture; the very idea, however unphilosophical, that is presented to us of the present earth as *an immense ruin* to be finally consumed by the volcanos without, the combustible materials within, the sun opening a passage to its *central fire*, and the earthquakes that unhinge its deepest foundations;—these are thoughts whose formation indicates vigorous intellectual exertion; and a strength corresponding to

that

that of the causes, whose co-operating influence will effectuate the destruction of the frame of nature *!

The force with which sentiments in the conduct of an extensive plan impress the mind, depends upon circumstances that vary according to the purpose which the writer hath ultimately in view. Political observations on the manners of an age, are strenuously conveyed to the mind when there is nothing peculiarly emphatical in the expression, when an enumeration is made of the different ideas which the same objects excite in men animated by virtuous emulation, or enervated by luxurious effeminacy.—" I have often heard
" (says Sallust) that Quintus Maximus,
" Publius Scipio, and other eminent
" members of the republic, used to say,
" that when they gazed upon the statues
" of their ancestors, their minds were most
" vehemently excited to the practice of
" virtue. Not that the wax, or the figure

---

*See particularly the two Dissertations upon the Deluge, and the Conflagration.

" into

"into which it was moulded, possessed so
"much power. But the memory of their
"illustrious actions, imprinted by this
"conveyance an idea so forcible and per-
"manent upon the breasts of these great
"descendants, as never to be effaced until
"the same virtue had rendered their fame
"as extensive, and their glory equally
"complete.—But, on the other hand, (con-
"tinues this historian) who is there of
"us all, tainted as we are by corrupted
"manners, whose emulation extends any
"further than to the riches and magni-
"ficence of our ancestors? Probity and
"action are out of the question. Even
"men of mean birth, who formerly ac-
"quired distinguished pre-eminence by
"their virtue, obtain in these times the
"first dignities of the state; more by
"theft and robbery, than by any com-
"mendable occupation *." We have
here

---

* "Sæpe audivi ego Quintum Maximum, Publium Scipionem, præterea civitatis nostræ præclaros viros solitos ita dicere: quum majorum imagines intuerentur, vehementissime animum sibi ad virtutem accendi:
scilicet

here a strong picture set before us of the degenerate manners of the Romans in our historian's age. The particular example selected of effects produced on the minds of men in his, and in a former age, from viewing the statues of their predecessors, is happily chosen for this end; and without any exterior ornament of diction, conveys a more forcible idea of a people universally emasculated by luxury, than the pomp of rhetorical declamation could ever have presented.—Let us hear Demosthenes on the same subject.—" It is not (says he) " surprising that a warlike, active, inde- " fatigable prince, (Philip) should conquer " a people who are suspended and irre- " solute. I wonder not at this. It would

---

scilicet non ceram illam neque figuram tantam vim in sese habere: sed memoria rerum gestarum eam flammam egregiis viris in pectore crescere, neque prius sedari quam virtus eorum famam atque gloriam adæquaverit. At contra, quis est omnium his moribus quin divitiis & sumptibus, non probitate neque industria cum majoribus suis contendat?—Etiam homines novi qui per virtutem soliti erant nobilitatem antevenire, furtim, & per latrocinia potius quam bonis artibus ad imperia & honores nituntur." Salust. Jugurth. in proem.

" be

"be surprising, indeed, if you, who do
"nothing in war, should conquer an
"enemy who is attentive to all its ope
"rations. This, Athenians, is astonishing,
"that you, who once attacked the people
"of Lacedæmon in defence of the liberty
"of Greece; who generously transferred
"to others those emoluments which you
"might have detained for your own use;
"that you, in short, who braved with
"such intrepidity the dangers of war in
"their cause, should now exert yourselves
"so indolently in your own! that having
"risked every thing formerly to save
"others, you now behold your own li
"berty, and your own possessions, in the
"most imminent hazard, and are doing
"nothing to preserve them *." In these
examples

---

* Ου δη θαυματεον εςιν ει ςρατευομενος, και πονων
εκεινος αυτος, και παρων εφ' απασι, και μηδενα καιρον
μηδ'ωραν παραλειπομενος, ομως μελλοντων, και ψη
φιζομενων, και πυνθανομενων περιγιγνεται. Ου δη
θαυμαζω τυτο εγω.—Τυναντιον γαρ ην θαυμασον ει
μηδεν ποιυντες ημεις αν τοις πολεμυσι προσηκει τα
παντα ποιυντος α δει περιημεν.—Αλλ' εκεινο θαυμαζω,
"

examples we observe and are impressed wholly by the sentiment, which acquires such strength from the comparison here carried on, as must have been felt universally, whatever expression had been selected to convey it. The correspondence of this last circumstance is an improvement to which we attend afterwards with satisfaction, when we observe the propriety with which embellishment of every kind is avoided in it, as the effect of so forcible and interesting an application must at least have been weakened by such an attempt, if not in a great measure superseded.

In the conduct of philosophical investigation a thought acquires strength, and the impression made by it is rendered dur-

---

ει Λακεδαιμονιοις μεν ποτε ω Ανδρες Αθηναιοι υπερ των ΕΛΛΗΝΙΚΩΝ ΔΙΚΑΙΩΝ αυτηρατε, και πολλα ιδια πλεονεκτησαι πολλακις υμιν εξον ουκ εθελησατε αλλ' ινα οι αλλοι τυχωσι των δικαιων τα υμετερα αυτων ανελισκετε εισφεροντες, και προεκινδυνευετε ςρατευομενοι. Νυν δε οκνειτε εξιεναι, και μελλετε εισφερειν υπερ των υμετερων αυτων κτηματων. Και της μεν αλλης σεσωκατε ΠΟΛΛΑΚΙΣ ΠΑΝΤΑΣ, και καθ' εκαςον εν μερει. Τα δε ΥΜΕΤΕΡΑ αυτων απολωληκοτες καθησθε. ΔΗΜΟΣΘ. Ολυνθια, κεφ. β.

able when its energy is displayed in a climax justly constituted, the parts of which are distinct, and the procedure rational. A frivolous question connected remotely with such a thought, but whose nature has not been sufficiently comprehended, is shown likewise in a clearer and stronger light, by being simply repeated after having carried on such a representation, than by any other method adopted for this purpose. It is difficult to separate upon many occasions, questions that minister wholly to curiosity, from such as tend to convey real information; and even when this distinction is made, the former must be placed in a very conspicuous point of view, in order to deter men stimulated by a powerful passion from engaging in enquiries that can be brought to no satisfactory conclusion, though the mind is flattered in a very different manner when these are first set before it. How many profound metaphysical speculations of no emolument to the reader, who receives disgust instead of instruction from their perusal, and of great detriment to the author,

thor, who, by launching beyond his depth, has made no other difcovery than the defect of his own underftanding; how many of thefe might have been avoided, had the perfons employed in them felt the effect of the following nervous reafoning of the Roman philofopher; which fhows the frivolous nature of the fubjects that have fo long engroffed their attention! After having, in general, obferved of the mind, that whatever fubftance that is which feels, thinks, lives, and animates the body, it muft be celeftial, and confequently eternal; he illuftrates his reafoning by faying, that even the Deity himfelf we conceive only to be a Being difengaged from all material obftruction, endowed with a principle of eternal motion, which he communicates to all things. Of this kind (fays he) and of the fame nature is the human mind.—
" But (replies fome *minute* enquirer) where
" is this mind, and what is it after all?—
" Apply (fays our illuftrious philofopher)
" thefe queftions to thy own foul.—Canft
" thou anfwer them?—No.—But becaufe
" I have not received every faculty I
would

" would *wish* to poffefs, doft thou, there-
" fore, forbid me to make ufe of fuch as
" are really conferred on me?—What the
" mind perceives not, its own form or
" appearance is of leaft confequence. It
" perceives, undoubtedly, at all times
" ftrength, fagacity, memory, action, ce-
" lerity.—Thefe objects are great, divine,
" eternal. After knowing thus much
" of its nature, queftions that regard its
" countenance, and place of refidence, are
" not worth an anfwer *."

In this noble paffage the author diftinguifheth, with true philofophical fagacity, the ufeful from the trifling and abfurd in an enquiry of the greateft importance; and by a climax well-conducted, when he enforceth the firft mentioned objects (hæc

---

* " Ubi igitur, & qualis eft ifta mens?—Ubi *tua* & *qualis?*—Potefne dicere? An fi omnia ad intelligendum non habeo quæ habere vellem; ne his quidem quæ habeo mihi per *te* uti licebit?—Non videt animus quod minimum eft fuam formam.—Vim certe fagacitatem, memoriam, motus, celeritatem videt. Hæc magna, hæc divina, hæc fempiterna funt.—Qua facie quidem fit, aut ubi habitet ne quærendum quidem eft." Tufcul. Difput. lib. i. cap. 28.

magna,

magna, hæc divina, hæc sempiterna sunt), impresseth as powerfully upon the mind a conviction of their utility, as of the frivolous nature of the others rendered more conspicuous by being placed in opposition. Uniting, therefore, the distinct characters of a philosopher and an orator, he forcibly inculcates those truths as an eloquent writer, which as a philosopher he discerned to have importance.

II. Thus far we have considered the character of just Composition, here examined, as influencing various kinds of sentiment, when unaccompanied with any uncommon energy of diction, or strength of illustration. When these last concur with the former, as well in disposition as in degree, the combination is perfect, and is known by the vigour and permanence of its impression. It is true, indeed, that a sentiment strongly conceived communicates a corresponding emphasis to expression at all times, in the same manner as a passion powerfully excited, gives ardor and vivacity to the countenance. In certain instances, when a detail becomes deeply

deeply interesting, and when an address is pointed to the heart, no art, unless it is very refined, ought (as we have already shown *) to be made use of. A few simple words, just inspired by the occasion, produce the full effect to be brought about in such circumstances as these; and an attempt to amplify or illustrate, would either weaken or subvert it. A man, feeling the pressure of some great affliction, will make use of few words. But the two extremes of perfect indifference, or absolute despair, adopt none at all. A masterly writer, therefore, will in the first case employ few strokes, though these significant and strongly expressive. In conducting a passion to the last excess, he will know that all description hath a boundary assigned to it; and by acting like the painter, who gave various expressions to the persons attending the sacrifice of Iphigenia, but veiled the face of her father, he will finish a picture incomparably more animated in such instances, than language and images could make out.

---

* Vol. I. sect. vii. Note.

But

But thefe obfervations relating to a few particular and very fingular cafes, though they could not with any propriety have been omitted, yet have no weight when referred to the more ufual fubjects of Compofition, in which thoughts that are recommended intrinfically rather by their ufe than their novelty, and which though approved by the power of underftanding, yet imprefs but flightly that of memory when retailed in unornamented expreffion, acquire peculiar fignificance by being conveyed in emphatical language, or preffed home by appropriated and ftriking illuftration. It is principally by means of this energy, communicated to the *ftyle* of Compofition, that the two arts of eloquence and poetry make impreffions more vigorous and permanent than any other. Nor ought the advantages derived from this circumftance to be confidered by the difpaffionate philofopher, as even of fecondary confequence, far lefs as frivolous and unneceffary. If we allow that he is the moft ufeful member of fociety, whofe thoughts by being ftrenuoufly inculcated are

are moſt univerſally uſeful, a man who is capable in this manner of effectuating ſuch a purpoſe is in every valuable ſenſe preferable to him whoſe ſentiments, however excellent in themſelves, are enervated by feeble expreſſion, or rendered dry by being defectively illuſtrated.

It is univerſally acknowledged, that genius never commands admiration more powerfully than when it is employed in giving ſuch ſignificance to an uſeful precept; or common ſentiment, as by ſeizing the faculty of imagination makes a durable impreſſion upon that of remembrance. When a thought is truly ſublime, or is ſtrongly marked by its originality, we expect to meet with a correſponding energy in the diction, and look upon this as a neceſſary accompaniment. But the mind exerts a creative energy that is contemplated with aſtoniſhment when we find it giving diſtinction to every idea that falls under its cogniſance; and when ſuch thoughts as we have often met with, and have as frequently neglected, are improved by paſſing through this intellectual alembic ſo as to influence conduct.

In order to produce the purposes here mentioned, it ought by no means to be considered as necessary, that we make use, upon all occasions, of the figures or idioms of poetry. These, it is no doubt true, when adapted to their objects with propriety, contribute as much as any other means to accomplish it effectually. Though an important expedient, however this is not an only one, and its use, though indispensable upon some occasions, would be unsuitable in many cases, and injudicious. Thoughts, when considered as forming in various combinations the parts of a comprehensive plan to be detailed in Composition, will naturally be viewed either as supporting each other in a connected series when the argumentation is closely carried on, or as standing more loose and detached, when a question may require to be illustrated, and to be exposed in a variety of lights. In the first case, it is requisite, above all other circumstances, in order to convey each of these as strongly as possible to the mind, that the author

author should make use of as few words as may be consistent with that perspicuity which ought to be his ultimate aim. Metaphors he may and ought to adopt, because these, when well applied, render an argument clear and forcible at the same time. But while he is not sparing of this figure, a judicious writer will study to use it in the present instance, only when the idea thus enforced would have otherwise been obscure, or so unimportant as not to have fixed attention*. Nor is it injurious

to

---

* I know no work, either ancient or modern, in which the figure here recommended is introduced with greater force and propriety than in the excellent work of Quintilian, to which we have so frequently referred. This admirable critic, seems to have understood thoroughly both their nature and their use in Composition. We have already considered his definition of a metaphor, and have shown its justness. In the sixth chapter of his eighth book, the curious reader will find him treating this subject at great length, and illustrating his remarks by numerous examples. To this, therefore, we refer him. Let us only observe, how justly he has himself exemplified his own rules. He says of this figure in general, that when admitted properly into Composition it

conveys

to the reputation of any author, however eminent, to affirm, that in a work of length, particularly of the argumentative kind, many such ideas must necessarily be admitted. In the proof of every hypothesis, however paradoxical, the principles to which the mind originally recurs in order to establish a conclusion, must be such as are universally intelligible; and

---

conveys an idea more forcibly than the words in whose room it is placed. " Metaphora plus valere debet eo quod expellit." Instit. lib. ii. c. 3. He mentions it likewise as a means to render an object clear and intelligible. Lib. viii. cap. 6. Among many other passages of his work, which might here be adduced as proofs of the conformity that takes place betwixt his rules and his practice, the following, in which both purposes are accomplished at once, is remarkable. " Nec mirum (says he, speaking of the action of an orator) si esta quæ tamen in *aliquo* sunt posita *motu* tantum in animis valent, quum pictura *tacens opus*, & *habitus* semper *ejusdem* sic in intimos penetret affectus, ut ipsam vim dicendi nonnunquam superare videatur." Instit. lib. xi. cap. 3. Nothing can be more appropriated and forcible, than the language and illustration employed here. How vividly is the mind impressed with the effect arising from the *real action* of a consummate orator, perpetually varying when it recollects the impression made upon it by one single attitude imitated in painting!

he,

he, who in a philofophical difquifition calculated perhaps upon the whole to let in new light upon the mind, fhould expect to be entertained by the novelty of thefe contemplated feparately without regard to the ultimate purpofe, would form an expectation that can never be gratified. It is not fo much to the firft principles laid down (which cannot be too fimple and obvious) that we attend, as to their difpofition and tendency to effectuate a certain end. As we are apt, however, to be fatigued by following out thefe at length, which make of themfelves no very ftrong impreffion, it is of great confequence to an author, that his diction be rendered peculiarly emphatical in this cafe, by a choice of fignificant words, and by the beauty of expreffive metaphors happily interwoven (if we may thus term it) in the compofition, that thefe may be read with attention, and recollected with facility.

We have, in a former fection, adduced an example of Compofition, diftinguifhed

at

at the same time by strength and simplicity in historical narration *. It is difficult to illustrate, in the same manner, our observations on the most proper method of rendering expression nervous in the conduct of an argumentative detail; because such examples, in order to be complete, would run into too great length. Observe, however, in what manner one of the greatest masters of language, among the ancients, at the same time elucidates and enforceth a maxim by no means remarkable for its novelty; but rendered extremely so by the expressive words that are selected to convey it. Speaking of the persons that are best qualified for the purpose of education, our author says,—" Inprimis evitandus, & in pueris præcipue magister aridus, non minus quam teneris adhuc plantis siccum & sine humore ullo solum. Inde fiunt humiles statim & velut terram spectantes qui nihil supra quotidianum sermonem attollere audeant.—Macies illis pro sanitate, & judicii loco infir-

---

* Book II. sect. ii.

mitas

mitas est.—Quare mihi ne maturitas quidem ipsa festinet, nec musta in lacu statim austera fiat," &c. Quintil. Instit. lib. ii. c. 4. It is by metaphors thus happily blended with the thought, and coalescing with it, as it were, that every object becomes dignified and significant; and we are led to admire the genius of one man, endowed with this distinguishing talent, in the expression of those very ideas which in a performance divested of it would be deemed vulgar or insignificant. In many cases, however, it is no doubt neither proper nor indeed practicable to preserve this figured diction, particularly when a few obvious truths are laid down in the language wholly unornamented as the basis of an hypothesis. The safest method of rendering Composition nervous in such instances, is to make use of as few words as the nature of the subject will admit, and to avoid enlargements when not absolutely necessary. A writer of good sense never discovers this quality more obviously, than by appearing always to know when he has just said enough. Redundant epithet be he will shun, as enervating what it is applied to strengthen, and declamation as relaxing attention, which is kept up by observing the end of a certain research, advancing nearer as we proceed, and more as it were, within our reach. A subject, treated upon these principles, will please by coherence, when not distinguished by vigour of sentiment; and language, where it cannot obtain the character of remarkable force, will yet have significance by gaining that of propriety.

Thus far we have considered the subject of this section, as improving the effect of sentiments that stand in close connection, and appear with the greatest possible advantage in consequence of well-adapted expression.

When the former, however, either have greater energy themselves, or admit in certain instances of more copious and forcible illustration, a defect of strength in the style of an author's Composition becomes conspicuous, in proportion as its prevalence is required as expedient or necessary. This character of the art, as appro-

appropriated more particularly to one species of it than to another, and constituted by different means when the objects vary to which it is applied, we shall have occasion afterwards to examine. Some general observations on these at present, it may here be proper to introduce.

1. It was formerly remarked, when we treated of the grand in Composition, that an object is often *rendered* sublime by an happy disposition of some preceding circumstances *. This we then attempted to confirm by examples. But the arrangement of previous ideas, though it will show us in any work whatever at what time the thought ought to have strength, and the diction corresponding energy; and in consequence of this discovery will make us immediately sensible when either or both is deficient, yet imparts not vigour as in the preceding instance it may do sublimity to an object. Yet by raising our expectations, it renders us particularly conscious of that weakness in the mind of

---

* Sect. v.

an

an author to which we owe a difappointment. Thus a philofopher expofing the futility of an objection, an hiftorian relating a defperate engagement, an orator fumming up his various arguments in an appeal required to be pointed, particular, and forcible; thefe gratify our hope indeed, when they acquit themfelves properly; but it is not to the difpofition of preceding circumftances that either the thought or expreffion owes its energy. It is wholly to the real force of the one, and to the correfponding propriety of the other, both which we examine apart. The fentiments of Socrates, therefore, communicated to his judges after he had been condemned to drink the hemlock, acquire fublimity from his peculiar fituation. We confider this circumftance, and pronounce thefe to be exalted. But when we come to examine the force of his reafoning, and the words he makes ufe of as juftly or unequally adapted, it is quite another matter. We drop immediately every thought of his fituation, and are impreffed only by the objects then contemplated.

It ought likewise to be observed, that the sublimity which owes its origin to a certain arrangement of previous incidents admits of degrees. It is true, indeed, that we expect the thoughts as well as the conduct of a great mind tried with adversity, to be dignified and consistent. But should these (the former particularly) be noble, though not astonishing, we still, with truth, denominate them sublime. It is otherwise when we consider vigour of intellect, as indicated by certain ideas, conveyed with suitable emphasis of language. When an expectation of this kind is once raised, the least failure in gratifying it is deemed to be a weakness. The philosopher, historian, or orator, who should fail to exert some part of that energy which his subject might necessarily demand, or the reader expect from his manner of conducting it, would be deemed unequal to the task he had undertaken to execute, and disqualified to rise with becoming vigour to his work,—Let us try an example.

When

When Isocrates has endeavoured to persuade Philip, in the oration addressed to this monarch, to bring about a general good understanding among the states of Greece, with whom at that time he was living in amity, we expect that he will immediately propose some motive of powerful efficacy, to make him follow an admonition apparently so contrary to his interest. But instead of meeting with any thing of this kind at the time we naturally look for it,—after having told him, that by following the counsel he had given him, " he would at the same time conciliate the " Greeks, and terrify the Barbarians *," our author makes a florid and elaborate panygeric on himself, who, in thinking rightly, and in directing to proper and honourable means, is inferior, he informs us, to no man whatever †.—Every reader

must

---

* Ην τα τοιαυτα προαιρη πραττειν εξον, τοις μεν Ελλησιν εση πιςος, τοις δε βαρβαροις φοβερος. ΙΣΟΚ. προς Φιλιπ. Λογ.

† Το δε φρονειν ευ, και πεπαιδευσθαι καλως (ει και τις αγροικοτερον ειναι φησει το ρηθεν) αμφισβητων και

θειην

must be sensible that there is great weakness in this conduct. It answers no purpose

Θειην αν εμαυτον εκ εν τοις απολελειμμενοις, αλλ' ιν τοις προεχουσι των αλλων. Id. ibid. This discourse of Isocrates has, I know, been greatly applauded in general; and one of the best ancient critics, Dionysius Halicarnasseus, recommends it as proper to be read by princes, to instil into their hearts the love of virtue. The tendency of some excellent moral observations in it to promote this purpose, we shall by no means dispute. It is only censured here as a Composition defective in strength of thought, and which sinks at that time when we expect the most vigorous and masterly execution. With regard to the arguments by which our author proposeth afterwards to convince Philip of the utility of his proposal, apposite as these have been judged to the accomplishment of this end, we will not be surprised upon reflection, that these made no strong impression on the mind of the Macedonian. What is his scheme taken altogether? After conciliating the attachment of all the Greek cities by offices of friendship, he exhorts this prince to march into Asia, and subdue the Persian nation. But this, surely, was not a plan likely to be prosecuted by Philip, who knew well that as long as Greece itself was left unsubdued, no professions of alliance from that quarter were to be depended upon. Jealous of its liberty, and of the ambition of this enterprising prince, Greece he was well aware would have obstructed instead of forwarding his design, as expecting, like the mouse in the fable, that after having devoured the *greater* objects, the lesser would fall an easy

pose but that of exciting disgust, and of prejudicing us, as we have observed him to do in a former instance, against every thing he afterwards advanceth on the subject. Strength of intellect (however conspicuously a character may be marked by vanity) will upon such an occasion be dis-

---

easy prey to his rapacity. His insincerity was too well known to make his promises be regarded as of any consequence. Philip, therefore, pursued a much better plan than that proposed to him here by Isocrates: which was, to put it beyond the power of his enemies at home to give him disturbance, before he thought of carrying the war into a foreign empire. The events that fell out upon the death of this great prince, after he had effectuated this purpose, clearly show us what measures the states of Greece would have adopted had he left them at liberty by marching sooner into Asia. Debilitated as they they were, they forgot in a moment the loss of Cheronæa, and the same people who had chosen Philip their generalissimo, took arms against Alexander. Should it be said that the Greeks had at last been driven by force to take that course with regard to the former, which they might formerly have adopted from choice; I have already shown that this would never have been the case, from their opinion of this man's insincerity. These remarks, though foreign to the present subject, the author hopes that his readers will excuse, as being naturally suggested by the mention of this celebrated oration.

covered

covered by ſtrenuous argumentation, and by motives (whether concluſive or not,) yet enforced as powerfully as the nature of the ſubject would admit.

The proof adduced here of intellectual debility, exhibits it principally as influencing the ſentiment and conduct of a diſcourſe. We obſerve it to take place in the diction, more particularly when an author, after having acquitted himſelf properly in conducting the ſubordinate branches of his theme, fails juſt at the moſt important criſis of uſing that " verbum ardens," that language full of energy, by which we then expect his Compoſition to be diſtinguiſhed in all caſes, or thoſe picturesque and animated images which ought more particularly to predominate in the ſpheres of eloquence and poetry. It would be endleſs to adduce examples in proof of this remark, as the reader of taſte may collect many for himſelf, both from ancient and modern performances. We may obſerve, however, that the diſpoſition of previous circumſtances prevents us from being pleaſed, even with moderate execution

tion at fuch a time, becaufe from thefe we have naturally been led to expect fomething higher. When after having brought his argument to a period, a philofopher comes to place the whole in one confiftent fummary before the mind; when after having expofed the falfhood of a plaufible reprefentation, he proceeds to examine its confequences, we confider him as deficient in ftrength of conception and of feeling, whofe ideas are not then conveyed with fuch emphafis as produceth at once a very fenfible and permanent effect. The fame remark may be applied to the hiftorian, whofe indignation we fuppofe to be roufed by having recorded an infamous tranfaction; and in fimilar cafes to the orator, and the poet.

However, therefore, in certain circumftances that conduct may be deemed great which rifeth not to the wonderful, yet when ftrength, either of language or of fentiment, is necefsarily required, we make no allowance as in the other cafe for defect in either, which is immediately fuppofed to indicate a mind whofe feelings are weak, or whose powers are disproportioned to their subject. What is the cause for which we judge so differently of these characters of Composition?—Upon recollection we shall find it to lie in the ends which these propose separately to accomplish.—The sublime (we have already seen) is always directed to raise *admiration*. Whatever object excites this passion we contemplate as great; but the imagination, which principally takes cognisance of it, without being exalted to its highest sphere, may yet be raised to a superior one, and betwixt the dignified that awakes, and the astonishing that holds it in almost viewless exstasy, there are many degrees that constitute (if we may thus express it) the range of *the sublime*. Expectation, therefore, even when excited in the highest degree, may be in some measure disappointed when an idea though not reaching the first, yet falls not beneath the lowest step of this scale, and is still regarded as noble, though by no means astonishingly exalted.—But it is otherwise with the nervous in Composition, of which the

heart,

heart, not the imagination, decides; and of whose defect, when it is expected eminently to predominate, we are rendered sensible by *feeling*. Here there are no other degrees than those that are prescribed by the nature of the subject. We expect not, for instance, that Plato should convey his arguments with the same energy with which Homer sets before us the deeds of Achilles. But when once we are interested thoroughly in a question, a reflection that might have significance in one connection, is wholly uninteresting in another, and an image of unquestioned energy, when applied to some circumstances, will be censured in others, as weak, and unappropriated *.

A

---

* In conducting a work, composed of very complicated members to a period, to expect that *equal* energy of mind should be displayed upon every occasion when this may, no doubt, be necessary, would be idle and extravagant. Of all authors whatever, *Homer* is perhaps the least defective of this quality in general. Yet amidst that amazing variety of objects pourtrayed in the Iliad, need we wonder if we sometimes meet with an image comparatively weak at least, and inadequate to its original ?—One instance of this kind
it

A writer of discernment, therefore, ought to be particularly cautious, lest in the

it may be to the present purpose to select. When Achilles, in the twenty-first book of the Iliad, engages in a combat, fruitful of new and astonishing events, with the river Scamander, the genius of the stream is represented as raising it from the bottom, and attempting to overwhelm this formidable enemy, by loading his waves with the carcases with which he had choaked up the tide. Achilles seizeth a tree, born down by the current, and leaps from it on the shore. But the god attacks him on all sides. To convey an idea of the inundation bursting every where on his head, Homer makes use of the following image.
"As when a labouring man brings a rill of water
"from its fountain to refresh his plants, and beautify
"his garden, holding the line in his hand, and clear-
"ing the passage with his spade, on a sudden the
"waters streaming before him down the declivity
"throw the pebbles into confusion, and instead of
"following, go before their leader.—So with what-
"ever rapidity Achilles flew, Scamander, still swifter,
"rolled his billows before him." ΙΔΙΑΔ. φ. α.
l. 257. This illustration has undoubtedly great beauty. It gives an entertaining variety to the narration, and (what is not always the case with Homer's images) is adapted to its object in every circumstance. But with all these advantages in its favour, if it is true (as we have endeavoured to prove at some length, sect. v.) that the image which is employed to set a great action or personage before our eyes, ought to *exceed* rather than fall short of the original, we shall then

the original choice of his subject he should fix upon one demanding a more strenuous exertion of intellect than that to which his mind is adequate; because there is not one among all the characters of Compo-

---

then pronounce this to be defective as a forcible representation. For though a stream defeating the intention of the labourer who means to scoop out a channel for it, by overflowing the grounds before him, represents to us Achilles surrounded by the Scamander, whose waves retarded his pursuit of the Trojans, and were before him wherever he went;—yet surely the rill that waters a garden defeating the purpose of a husbandman, is an image as disproportioned to the impetuous Scamander guided by a God, charging its billows with heaps of dead, and breaking on the head of Achilles, as the husbandman himself standing with his spade in his hand, and seeing his work overwhelmed by the water, is inferior to this hero leaping on the shore, and springing at every bound from this divinity as far as a warrior can throw a spear.—The illustration, therefore, is here inadequate to its original in point of strength. The circumstances of the former, though beautiful when contemplated alone, yet shrink into nothing when placed in comparison with the latter. These are appropriated, but not picturesque. If, however, a defect of this kind can never be excused, it must surely be pardoned in such a work as the Iliad, in which an imagination, kept perpetually on the stretch, has erred as seldom in this way as it ever did in any case, when not guided by inspiration.

sition,

fition, whofe deficiency is fooner obferved, even in a flight degree, than this of *vigorous* execution; nor is there any for which when once detected, a performance is more univerfally cenfured. When our expectation is carried to a certain height, either from the nature of the theme itfelf, or from the manner in which it is conducted, we become perfectly fenfible of an author's weaknefs, who, though adequate to every inferior reprefentation, falls off when engaged in the moft important; and by fubftituting affected, in place of natural energy, difcovers the debility of talents improperly exerted, which in a fphere better adapted to their exercife, might have been employed with propriety and emolument. On the contrary, however, it ought to be obferved, that as a certain previous arrangement of ideas renders a defect of ftrength, either in thought or expreffion, remarkably perceptible to a man of difcernment, fo when the execution is adequate in this character to the fubject, the circumftance above-mentioned contributes equally to render us fenfible of its

full

full effect. Memory is never more permanently impressed, than when expectation is succefsfully gratified; and an author, who in the developement of his plan exerts an energy proportioned to the occasion, at the same time that he riseth in his reader's estimation, effectuates a purpose by the significance given to every object, which the same representation less strenuously enforced, or placed in another connection could never have accomplished.

2. As a writer, therefore, whose composition is distinguished as nervous or forcible, may render this character perfectly conspicuous, by bringing on that *crisis* in his discourse at which it is required most particularly to predominate; so in order to preserve it univerfally as much as the nature of a subject will admit, he ought to select as often as possible, lively and appropriated illustrations. It would be wholly useless to enlarge here upon these as communicating peculiar energy to sentiments, and even rendering their influence at sometimes irresistible; because we have already discussed this branch of our
subject

subject at considerable length. We shall therefore, only observe at present, with regard to the *strength* which these give to Composition, that two things are requisite to constitute this character. 1ft. That the image should either be really stronger than the object to which it is applied, or at least should be supposed to exceed it in this respect. 2dly, That foreign or adventitious circumstances, should, if possible, be wholly avoided in the application, or admitted as separately as possible.

That an illustration ought usually to exceed its original pattern in strength, to convey a forcible, as much as in grandeur to constitute a sublime representation, will be acknowledged upon the principles formerly enumerated. As it is the business of every writer to interest his readers in the subject of which he treats, those images which are called in particularly to animate his narration, ought to exceed the objects in strength which these are brought to illustrate, in order to supply, in some measure, the loss of *ocular evidence*, to which all narration is inadequate. When

Observations on Composition. 239

an illuftration, in the fame manner, is appropriated to a *fentiment*, which in a certain connection hath peculiar emphafis, we are fo far from condemning the author for mixing *bolder* ftrokes in his illuftration than we might conceive the original to have fuggefted, that we look upon thefe as indications of mafterly execution. Thefe rules may be deemed perhaps at firft view not to be applicable to every cafe, and therefore to be imperfect. A fentiment (it may be faid with truth) fometimes acquires great ftrength from an image purpofely reprefented, as inferior to its original, inftead of being ftronger or more expreffive. Thus in Shakefpeare's beautiful Ode,

> Blow, blow, thou winter wind!
> Thou art not fo unkind
> As man's ingratitude, &c.

the two images of " winter wind," and " biting froft," difficult as thefe are often to be fupported, are yet denominated comparatively light, when compared with the ingratitude and inexcufable negligence of mankind, the two originals to which thefe

cor-

correspond. Yet the latter are strengthened by this comparison; and the whole is incomparably glowing and animated. But a discerning reader will take notice, that in every instance of this kind, without exception, the original object acquires force, not because the illustration is *really* of an inferior nature, but represented, though really higher in itself, as less than the thing to which it is compared, the one loseth no part of its original force, and the other gains a considerable accession. A mind, pained by the recollection of ingratitude, is very forcibly set before us when compared with a man feeling in a desart the blasting winds, and piercing frosts of winter; but while the consequences arising from these last, are placed full in our sight, the anguish, excited by the other, is painted with incomparable energy, when the poet, personifying the biting air, says,

> Thy *tooth* is not *so keen*,
> Thou causest not *that teen*;
> Although *thy breath be rude.*

The reader will easily supply to himself many other examples of the same kind, to which this observation may be applied.

The

The other rule we laid down for rendering images forcible when applied to thoughts in compofition, viz. that thefe without the embellifhment of adventitious circumftances, fhould be adapted with propriety to their objects, reflection will induce us to follow likewife as expedient. It is indeed true, that an image may be thus appropriated to its original without rendering it animated, in the fame manner as the colour that is fuited to the complexion of a countenance, may add no diftinguifhing vivacity to its expreffion. With regard to the firft, however, it is certainly true, that though this correfpondence betwixt an illuftration and its original pattern may take place (as we have already feen) when no degree of ftrength is communicated to either; yet when it is violated by the introduction of objects foreign to the principal purpofe, the force of both is confiderably leffened, and their impreffion is rendered lefs durable. The ufe of unappropriated circumftances in the illuftration of an important fentiment, hath the fame effect upon the mind of a reader

reader as the " turba verborum," (as Cicero calls it) the multitude of words. The ftyle of Compofition is enervated by both. The ftrength indeed of the image itfelf confidered apart from the language, depends, no doubt, upon that of the imagination which conceives it. This radical character, therefore, can be altered by no difpofition whatever. But the figure of Compofition here mentioned, when little detached ftrokes are admitted into it, by carrying the reader's attention away from the principal point, renders that diffufe which ought to have been clofely united; and impairs in this manner the effect of the whole.

Thefe obfervations it ought to be remembered, relate wholly to *fentiments* as energetically conveyed by illuftrations, in whatever fpecies of the art thefe may be introduced. With regard to action, (that high kind of it in particular which forms the epopœa) the matter is different. In a narration extremely diverfified, the images drawn promifcuoufly from all fources muft be at the fame time frequent and various,

as

as the circumstances direct to which these are applied. Amidst such diversity, the mind though pleased to find in each proportion and symmetry, yet requires to be relieved by strokes somewhat digressive. The force of a description, it is true, may be weakened in a small measure by this conduct at the time. But the writer, like an able commander, by extending his powers at some times over a larger compass than necessity might prescribe, will most successfully accomplish his ultimate purpose; and if a lively impression is made while these are yet diffused, it will become irresistible when they are close and concentrated. In an eloquent oration, therefore, and in the highest species of poetry, the diffusion here censured in general, may be judiciously adapted to promote a good end. In other branches of the art in general, particularly in the case formerly mentioned, it renders, as we have seen, Composition enervated.

III. We have now endeavoured to show at considerable length, what is implied in the epithet *nervous* when viewed as a character of Composition, what faculty takes cognisance of it, and by what circumstances it is constituted. Our observations on these subjects will enable us more easily to comprehend what remains to be treated; the causes that deprive language of its due force, and the most proper method of avoiding, or of correcting this weakness.

The causes that deprive expression of its just influence are principally the three following. 1. Improper diffusion of any kind, but more particularly the too frequent use of compounded epithets. 2. The unnecessary admission of the particles of speech into Composition, by whose use its dignity is lost, and its impression enfeebled. 3. When neither of these signatures characterise a performance, this defect of strength will still be conspicuous when either the subject in general, or any particular branch of it is disproportioned to the ability of the writer.

1. We have made use of the term *diffusion* frequently in this section, when the connection in which it stood must have rendered it sufficiently intelligible. We must

must here, however, explain it a little more minutely. We commonly observe, that the language adopted by a rich imagination is florid, copious, and luxuriant. With the epithet *copious* we associate no idea of enervated diction; but on the contrary, apply it to a work in which every successive object is presented before the mind in its complete proportions; and deem it justly, when eminently predominant, to be the most perfect character of Composition*. We call this the *most perfect character* of the art, because it is not, like any of those we have yet examined, required to predominate only or principally in certain species; but extends universally to all. A copious writer, in whatever department of literature his abilities are exerted, is one who does justice to every branch of his subject; and by saying all that can be advanced on it with propriety, fills at the same time the ear

---

* Εϛι Λεξις κρατιϛη πασων, η τις αν εχοι πλειϛας αναπαυλας τε και μεταβολας αρμονικς, οταν τυτο μενεν περιοδω λεγηται, τυτι δε εξω περιοδε. ΔΙΟΝΥΣ. ΑΛΙΚΑΡ. περι Συνθεσ. Ονομ. C. 28.

with

with the harmony of his periods, and gives the mind a satisfactory view of the theme of which he treats *.

A-kin

---

* The best critics, both ancient and modern, concur in recommending the use of this numerous diction, particularly to young persons, as much more eligible than the opposite character, even though verging on the extreme of verbosity. The reply of the poet Accius to Pacuvius, who allows his versification to be numerous and lofty, but censured it at the same time as defective in elegance, sets this remark in a very striking light.—" Ita est, inquit Accius, uti dicis, neque id sane me pœnitet, meliora enim fore quæ deinceps scribam. Nam quod in pomis est, itidem esse aiunt in ingeniis, quæ dura & acerba nascuntur, post fiunt mitia & jucunda: sed quæ gignuntur statim vieta & mollia atque in principio sunt uvida, non *matura* mox fiunt sed *putria*. Relinquendum igitur visum est in ingenio quod dies atque ætas mitificet." Aulus Gell. lib. xiii. cap. 2. Quintilian is very explicit on this subject. " Facile remedium est ubertatis, sterilia nullo modo vincuntur. Illa mihi in pueris natura nimium spei dabit in quâ ingenium judicio presumitur. Materiam esse primam volo vel *abundantiorem* atque *ultra quam oportet fusam*. Multum inde dement anni, &c." Instit. lib. ii. c. 4. The younger Pliny judges in the same manner of this character. " Delectare, persuadere, *copiam* dicendi spatiumque desiderant; relinquere vero aculeum in audientium animis is demum potest, qui non pungit sed infigit. Non enim amputata oratio & abscissa, sed *lata*, & *magnifica*, & excelsa tonat, fulgurat omnia

denique

Observations on Composition.

A-kin to this excellence, however, when subsisting in perfection, is that injudicious diffusion which we have mentioned as incompatible with vigorous execution*. It will

---

denique perturbat ac miscet." Epist. lib. i. epist. xx. A celebrated modern critic considers this subject very justly. His words deserve attention. " Absterreo (says he) juventutem a brevitate, cujus imitatio facillime ætatem hanc decipit. Juvenili ille brevitatis studio, aridus plerumque & exsuccus stylus evadit, nec facile ad *laudatam temperiem* venitur, nisi initio *libertas quædam* & *luxuries* fit quam ætas paulatim depascat." Lips. Epist.

* Cicero himself (as we are informed by Tacitus) escaped not the censure of his contemporaries, on account of this diffusion in his diction. " Satis constat nec Ciceroni obtrectatores defuisse quibus inflatus, & tumens, nec satis *pressus*; supra modum *exultans* & *superfluens*, & *parum Atticus* videretur. Legisti utique & Calvi, & Bruti ad Ciceronem missas epistolas ex quibus facile est deprehendere Calvum quidem Ciceroni visum exsanguem, &c. Rursumque Ciceronem a Calvo quidem mala audivisse tanquam *solutum & enervem*, a Bruti autem (ut ipsius verbis utar) tanquam fractum atque elumbem." De Orator. Dialog. Later ages, however, have done more justice to this admired ancient, whose language (if that of any writer ever deserved this panygeric) unites *the harmony* of the *copious*, with the *energy* of the *concise* in Composition; and may be denominated in words applied by an elegant poet to a noble river, " *full without overflowing.*" Denham. It is somewhat remarkable, that Tacitus himself,

will be immediately underſtood, by comparing theſe characters together, that as the copious in Compoſition is obtained when the full dimenſions of every object are diſplayed, ſo the diffuſe or verboſe takes place in it when in conſequence of an attempt to do more than is neceſſary theſe become diſproportioned. As ſoon as a writer verges from the point of perfection by falling into this error, his diction loſeth a part of its force, even while we are yet inſenſible of the cauſe, or are not ſo much affected as to trace it out with attention. A river, whoſe waters riſe to the higheſt level of its bank on either ſide, is a noble and majeſtic object upon which we dwell with admiration, and whoſe force is augmented in proportion as

---

himſelf, one of the moſt conciſe writers whom antiquity hath produced, recommends an expreſſion ſomewhat diffuſed, in treating ſerious ſubjects, to be made uſe of, particularly in annals. " Annalium tarda quædam eſt & iners ſcriptura." De Cauſis Corrupt. Eloq. c. 21. By the *tarda* and *iners* is here underſtood, that *copious* expreſſion which is neceſſary to convey ideas clearly to the mind, when many tranſactions muſt be ſuccinctly related.

the

the bounds approach to each other within which it is confined. But when its banks are either broken, or overflowed by the tide, the impetuofity of the current will be leffened as its range is extended, and the paffenger will ftem or repel it with more facility. Thus as the ftream is rude and turbulent when too much confined, fo when taking too wide a compafs it becomes languid and enervated. The application of this to the prefent fubject is obvious: the difficulty lies in preferving the juft medium.

In order to obtain this point, at leaft as nearly as poffible, a writer ought to avoid the *epithetical* ftyle as it may be termed, which is formed by the ufe of too many *adjectives* in a performance. Thefe, when introduced at all times as if the fubftantive ought never to ftand by itfelf, inftead of communicating ftrength to a difcourfe, render it, on the contrary, infipid and unmeaning. This is the cafe more particularly when thefe are either general, or are thrown in to fill up a period, and contain ufelefs repetitions. When Claudian introduceth

duceth his poem on the Rape of Proserpine, by saying,

> Inferni raptoris equos, afflataque curru
> Sidera Tenario, caligantesque profundæ
> Junonis thalamos, audaci promere cantu
> Mens congesta jubet.——

(words whose meaning cannot be adequately conveyed in a translation) the discerning reader will be sensible, that the sense of this passage is hurt by redundant epithets, which enfeeble the expression, while they render it inflated *. In the field

---

* The effect of this style will be more fully comprehended when it is compared either with an expression divested of epithet, or with one distinguished only by such as have propriety. We shall here produce an example of each. Atys recovering from the frenzy in which he had emasculated himself, and reflecting on his condition exclaims with great emotion,
Egone——
Patria, bonis, amicis, genitoribus abero?
Abero foro, palestra, studio, gymnasiis?
Miser, ah miser! Quærendum est etiam atque etiam
    anime
Quod enim genus? Figura est? Ego numquid abierim?
Ego Mulier?——
Jam, jam dolet quod egi, jam, jam quoque pœnitet.
                              Catul.
Here the reader will observe, that the poet attempts not

field of softer description; adjectives applied promiscuously in this manner to fill up a vacuity, as it would seem, constitute

not to heighten the distress of the scene by employing any epithet. Ideas are supposed to have poured too fast upon the mind to admit the heightening that ariseth from this circumstance. Atys speaks the language of nature, when he draws a comparison betwixt his past and present state in a few simple words, any of which would be weakened by the most forcible epithet that could be applied to it.—An instance of the last kind we shall take from Claudian himself, who, in the following beautiful lines, proposeth his subject with admirable simplicity, and makes not use of one epithet which could, with propriety, be altered or omitted.

 Sæpe mihi dubiam traxit sententia mentem
 Curarent superi terras, an nullus inesset
 Rector, & incerto fluerent mortalia casu.
 Nam cum dispositi quæsissem fœdera mundi,
 Præscriptosque maris fines, annique meatus,
 Et lucis, noctisque vices,—tunc omnia rebar
 Consilio firmata Dei.
 Qui variam Phœben alieno jusserit igne
 Compleri, solemque suo, &c. In Rufin. lib. i. ab init:

This might well pass as the language of the most accomplished author of the age of Augustus. The whole passage breathes the same spirit. We cannot transcribe it here. It is a happy specimen of the manner in which a philosophical subject ought to be proposed, in a style preserving the just medium betwixt bombast, and meanness; redundance, and defect.

the

the flowery, or puerile in Compofition, which indicates always either a weak, or an immature underftanding; and which nothing but youth and inexperience renders at any time excufable.

While we here condemn a ftyle that is *promifcuoufly* epithetical, it ought not to be imagined, that this circumftance ought to be wholly excluded from any fpecies of Compofition whatever; or even to be at all times fparingly introduced. A writer in profe, can never be faid to make ufe of too many adjectives in his work as long as thefe are not redundant, i. e. expreffive of the fame thing; but while each conveys a diftinct idea to the mind, and fuch as hath fignificance. In poetry, epithets can never weaken the diction of the writer while thefe are picturefque. But even in this cafe they fatigue the reader, by recurring upon him too often, and the *glare* of imagery is as apt to hurt a fufceptible mind, as the blaze of funfhine is to dazzle the eye. A man of genius will fucceed beft in rendering his work beautiful in the proper fenfe of that epithet, who knows

at

Observations on Composition.

at what time it is fit to restrain the luxuriance of his imagination; since excellence is constituted as much by the *judicious disposition* of *colours*, as by their *original invention*.

Compounded epithets are commonly made use of to place the original to which they are applied, in a point of view as striking and picturesque as it can possibly admit. For this purpose, the internal feelings of the heart, and abstracted ideas of the understanding, are illustrated by the union of two sensible objects to which we discover these to have some striking resemblance; and their originals are said to be *impersonated*, when rendered by an happy application of this kind cognisable by the senses, and pleasing to the imagination which is thus powerfully impressed. Thus fire-eyed anger, smooth-tongued flattery, pale-lip'd sorrow, rosy-featured ease, become much more significant by the combined epithets applied to them here, than by any single adjective of whatever import. Complexion, grace, attitude, and those circumstances in general that impress

the

the organs of sense, enter into the idea here placed before us, and render it at the same time lively and permanent. This figure, it must be acknowledged, hath been used much more frequently, and perhaps with greater success, by modern, than by ancient writers of eminence*. It constitutes,

---

* The *learned* reader must decide on the truth of this observation. Without confirming it, therefore, here by particular examination, which would far exceed the bounds we must prescribe to ourselves in this note, we shall only observe, that from the works of Homer, and Pindar, the capital Greek poets, and those of Virgil, the Roman, whose writings might afford examples of this character, we find but few instances of objects rendered picturesque by compounded epithet, in proportion at least to those which their subjects might have suggested. The epithets of this kind, applied by Homer to his heroes, are by no means the principal beauties of that immortal work. These are, in truth, neither very characteristical, nor much diversified. Hector is commonly distinguished by the two epithets of Κορυθαιολος, and Ανδροφονοιος, i. e. plume-shaking, and man-killing; Ulysses Πολυτρωπος, sometimes; and at others, both he and Achilles are distinguished by the general epithet of Διος. Agamemnon is called, with propriety though, Ευρυκρειων, wide-commanding. Even Achilles himself, is most commonly denominated Ποδυσωκυς, swift-footed;

tutes, however, when *placed with propriety*, one of the greatest beauties of poetry, (to which art it is peculiarly appropriated) and such as distinguisheth genius in its greatest eminence. But when in consequence of an affectation to attain this excellence at all times, it is applied indiscriminately to every object, its strength is impaired by this injudicious use of it; and figures which would have commanded admiration when contemplated apart, at proper intervals from each other, escape even observation by being thus presented in a promiscuous assemblage.

2. As Composition is thus weakened by diffusion and redundance of epithet, so

---

footed; which is often repeated, when the reader might expect that a much more forcible and picturesque phrase should be substituted in its room. There are, however, no doubt, some epithets wonderfully striking and happy in the Iliad. Pindar has some of the same kind, (examples of which cannot be selected here) but fewer, upon the whole, than it might be supposed that so great an imagination would have supplied. The case of Virgil we have already considered. It is probable, that the ancient poets in general, avoided making use of compounded epithets, as inconsistent with that *simplicity* of expression which they endeavour at all times to preserve.

it

it suffers in the same manner by the too frequent use of expletives, and of those monosyllabical particles which are employed to connect the parts of a sentence together. The effect of the first mentioned is most conspicuous in poetry, particularly when rhyme is adopted. In this case, the words *do, will, shall, have, had,* &c. applied to the corresponding tenses of verbs, render a poem like a pedant, at once stiff and unedifying, weak and affected. Pope at the same time exemplifies this fault, and expoſeth the effect of it.

<small>Expletives their feeble aid *do* join. Eſſ. on Crit.</small>

But let it be remembered, that this remark neither extends to dramatic poetry, nor to any species of Composition that approacheth to the looſer ſtyle of converſation. In these the expletives abovementioned have not only propriety, but ſignificance likewise in many caſes; becauſe inſtead of being introduced to fill up a sentence or a line, the whole force of it often rests upon the emphasis with which ſome of them are pronounced. When Iago ſays to Bianca, in the Moor of Venice,

Observations on Composition.

——— Guiltiness
Will speak, though tongues were out of use.

Lodovico to Othello, in the same play, when he had killed his wife,

You *shall* close prisoner rest.

The king of Denmark to Polonius, in Hamlet,

something's in his soul,
O'er which his melancholy sits in brood,
And I *do* doubt the hatch and the disclose
Will be some danger.

In these, and in many other examples of the same kind, an emphasis is laid on the expletive *shall, will, do,* which thus *give* energy to discourse, instead of *lessening* it, as in the first instance.

Prose Composition is weakened by nothing more effectually, than by the inconsiderate use of little particles, and monosyllables. These are like tools, which, when applied however apparently diminutive to a solid body, destroy its consistence, and break it into fragments. The little copulative AND in particular, when too frequently repeated, tends greatly to enervate a sentiment, and to destroy the harmony

mony of a period. On this account, the greatest masters of Composition frequently drop it altogether, when the sense is not injured by the omission; judging that the words expressive of certain ideas, when placed together in one view, have much more force without the repetition of this copulating particle, than with it.—" Non omnes (says the Roman orator) eos contemnunt de quibus male existimant. Nam quos improbos, maledicos, fraudulentos putant, &c. eos haud contemnunt quidem, sed de iis male existimant." Cicer. De Offic. The reader will observe, that the whole sentence is much more expressive when the terms *improbos*, &c. stand alone, than if the particle *et* had been applied to each of them, which, though an addition seemingly insignificant, would have impaired its strength as well as harmony *.—We avoid enlarging on this head,

---

* In the same manner our author, speaking a little after of the objects that give agreeable and painful sensations, says, " Voluptates, blandissimæ Dominæ, sæpe majores partes animi a virtute detorquent; & Dolorum

head, that our remarks may not be deemed too *minute.* Such as have been made, the subject appears not only to suggest as natural, but to demand as necessary.

3. We proceed, therefore, to observe, in the last place, that the cause most universally productive of an enfeebled expression, is a disproportion of the writer's abilities,

lorum cum admoventur faces, præter modum plerique exterrentur.—Vita, Mors, Divitiæ, Paupertas, omnes homines vehementissime permovent." Id. ibid. Here the sentiment is much more nervously expressed without the repetition of the copulative *et* adjected to the words *vita,* &c. than with this addition. The best classical writers avoid likewise at some times making use of the particle *aut* (or) in the comparison of things with each other. The repetition of the relative referring to a former person, renders a sentence incomparably more elegant and forcible. Thus Cicero, again, speaking of justice in its most enlarged acceptation, tells us.—" Nemo enim justus esse potest qui mortem, qui dolorem, qui exilium, qui egestatem timet." Id. ibid. This manner of representing the matter has a much greater efficacy, than if our author had said, as an inferior writer would have done, " aut dolorem, aut exilium," &c. The reader thrown into this track of observation, may extend it to many more instances than can be enumerated here, particularly in the English language, which abounds with monosyllables.

either to his subject in general, or to any particular branch of it.

When a theme in general demands more vigorous execution than that to which its author is adequate, the defect of strength is as conspicuous to a discerning eye, as the difference is to all betwixt the man who supports a considerable weight without difficulty, and him who heaves it from the earth with trepidation, totters in his gait every moment, and staggers with relaxed sinews, to the place at which it is to be deposited. The parts of a subject, when this is the case, commonly want that just coherence which constitutes a whole proportioned and consistent: the enlargements are either foreign or trifling; and those branches which are of least utility, and require the easiest exertion, lead the reader to form an expectation both from the author's promise, and from his execution, which, when brought to the trial, he is unable to gratify.

But as the defect of intellectual energy is thus rendered perfectly conspicuous when

when a theme is too great or comprehenfive for the mind that contemplates it, fo it often happens, that when no fuch defect takes place in general, yet a writer will difappoint expectation, not only in the delineation of a particular part, or in the ufe of a difproportioned illuftration, but even in his manner of treating a certain branch (perhaps an important one) of his fubject, demanding no greater proportion of mental ability than others to which he hath been found adequate. The firft mentioned of thefe, a good-natured reader will readily excufe. It is the characteriftic of every performance, and arifeth from the imperfection of human nature. Blemifhes of this kind are, perhaps, even neceffary to recommend the beauties of a performance, as the fhades of a picture fet off its graces to advantage. We may at leaft obferve, that a *perfect work* (could fuch a one be produced) would prefent a very uninterefting, if not a difagreeable object to that part of mankind, whofe enjoyment, if traced to its fource in the perufal

rufal of a performance, arifeth principally from the gratification of malevolence.

With regard to the other inftance of difproportioned vigour, that which appears in an author's way of treating a particular queftion, or branch of his difcourfe, in which he exerts not the fame ftrength, either of fentiment or expreffion, that he difplays upon every other topic; though it is a weaknefs much lefs excufable than the former, efpecially when arifing from want of attention; yet moft commonly it is only an indication that the mind of the writer is fitted to think with more perfpicacity, and to exprefs its ideas with greater energy, upon fome topics than upon others, which in the difcuffion of a comprehenfive plan will unavoidably fall out. That the operation of both cafes may be prevented as much as poffible, a man ought to reflect in the firft cafe, that in beftowing lefs attention on one part of his fubject than on another, he does injuftice to his reader, whofe judgment of its importance may be very different from his own; and in the laft he will moft fuccefsfully
rectify

rectify this inaptitude, by supplying in attention what he may want in natural propensity, and his thoughts, like a river diverted into an artificial bed, though diverged at first with difficulty from their native direction, will at last run freely in the channel that is opened to receive them.

IV. From the preceding observations on nervous Composition, as relating to sentiment, expression, and illustration; on the means that constitute this character of the art, and on the causes that deprive language of its energy, from these one truth will obviously appear to result;—that the first thing necessary to produce vigorous execution, is a perfect acquaintance with the subject of which we treat. There are, it is true, performances in whose composition there is apparently great strength, though the authors are found upon closer examination to have taken very defective views of their subjects. But when this is the case, it is usually the words or sounds, not the sense imparted in these, that seem to have emphasis. Language may, no doubt,

doubt, be swelled out to such an expression when the thought is wholly superficial; and, indeed, when the mind is conscious of a defect in sentiment, it naturally attempts to compensate this loss by far-fetched ornaments, and strenuous assertion. Men of imagination, in whom the faculty of understanding is either originally weak, or who have formed a very inadequate estimate of their subject, generally fall into the *declamatory* style, which though inconsistent with nervous Composition *in reality*, admits it greatly *in appearance*. Those on the other hand, whose view of their theme is equally incomplete, but who either *avoid* declamation, or *cannot* adopt it, bewilder themselves and their readers in the labyrinth of obscurity, and lose sight of *truth* in the pursuit of *distinction*. If it is true (as we have endeavoured to evince through the whole of this section), that the character here examined can only be said to obtain when the thought and the diction support and coalesce with each other, we can never ascribe it to any production in which the former is superficial.

The

The *declamatory*, and the *nervous* therefore, in the strict sense of the last epithet, are incompatible. The last-mentioned writers again, who " blunder about a meaning" which they cannot make out, far from deserving that the epithet *nervous* should be applied to their composition, distinguish it properly by no character but that of obscurity. Energy of expression is a secondary quality of the art here examined, derived from strength of sentiment, and always accompanying it. It is only when an author thoroughly comprehends the series of thoughts passing successively before him, that he will convey these with that masculine force which an idea strongly conceived will infuse, as it were, into his diction. Otherwise it may be tumid, ornamented, or diffuse; but never masterly and invigorated.

Cui *lecta potenter* erit *res*,
Nec *facundia* deseret hunc, neque lucidus ordo. Hor.

2. Some critics are of opinion, that the style of Composition in order to be denominated *nervous*, ought to be so concise and *close* (if we may thus express it) as to contain

contain juft the neceffary words that are expreffive of certain ideas, and no more. Such appears to be the meaning affixed to it by the detractors of Cicero, (mentioned in the celebrated Dialogue on the Corruption of Eloquence above referred to, when they accufe him of being defective in the *preſſus* and *atticus* *, as they denominate it. This manner is no doubt highly eligible when obtained in perfection. There are, however, two *capital* errors into which an author may be led by

---

* The ftyle here characterifed is probably termed *atticus* from the peculiar character of Demofthenical eloquence, which is diftinguifhed by an expreffion at the fame time remarkably concife, and happily appropriated. Ο δε ΔΗΜΟΣΘΕΝΙΚΟΣ ΛΟΓΟΣ ευτονος τη Φρασει, κεκραμενος τοις ηθεσι, και λεξεως εκλογη μεκοσμημενος, και χρωμενος ταξει τη κατα το συμφερον και μετα τε σεμνε την χαριν εχων και συνεχης· εις μαλιςα δικαςαι κατεχονται. ΔΙΟΝΥΣ. ΑΡΧΑΙΩΝ ΚΡΙΣ. Cicero looked upon the language of Demofthenes as fo remarkably energetical, that he characterifeth it by the fingle, but nervous epithet VIM. " Suavitatem Ifocrates, fubtilitatem Lyfias, acumen Hyperides, fonitum Æfchines, VIM Demofthenes habuit." De Orat. lib. iii.

attempt-

attempting it without proper attention;—
that of *harſhneſs*, and of *obſcurity*.

The harſh in Compoſition is conſtituted by words that have ſignificance thrown together without harmony. This happens either when there is no proper affinity betwixt the words employed in a diſcourſe, and the ſenſe conveyed in it; or when the ſtructure of periods is perplexed and diſſonant. Language may be ſaid to want a juſt correſpondence with the ſentiment (ſuppoſing this laſt to be ſtrongly conceived) when an attempt to maintain the harmony that ought to ſubſiſt betwixt theſe is carried too far; and by leaving out, as ſuperfluous, words that give ſoftneſs and elegance to expreſſion, an author collects together a ſet of unmuſical phraſes, by which the ear is ſhocked, and the ſenſe injured. We muſt not, however, ſo far miſtake the meaning of the term *harſh*, when applied to language, as to confound it with a *rough*, or even *rude* and *obſolete* phraſeology. The ſenſe, particularly in a well-wrought deſcription, may often require rough ſounds to be aſſembled, which

a juſt

a juſt diſpoſition will render harmonious *. Even rude and obſolete expreſſion in the ſame

---

* Every reader knows, that an aſſemblage of this kind conſtitutes one of the principal beauties of poetic expreſſion.

    Una eurusque, notusque ruunt, creberque procellis
    Africus——

and again,

    In ſegetem veluti cum flamma furentibus auſtris
    Incidit, & rapidus montano flumine torrens
    Sternit agros, &c.

Theſe deſcriptions, and many others of the ſame kind, far from being harſh or ungrateful, are, on the contrary, remarkably harmonious. The language of Spenſer in the ſame manner, and that of Taſſo, though rendered *obſolete* in ſome meaſure by time, are ſtill admired as elegant and melodious. Shall I be pardoned by the reader for giving an example of *harſh* Compoſition from the work of a modern author, whoſe writings in general are the ſtandards of harmonious expreſſion, as well as of philoſophical ſentiment?—Homer, deſcribing the preparations for the funeral of Patroclus, tells us, that the party ſent at a diſtance to collect wood for the pile, led their mules with difficulty over broken rocks, and precipices. The line

Πολλα δ'αναντα, καταντα, παραντα τε δ'οχμια τ'ηλθον.

hath great poetic beauty, but the tranſlation, in conſequence of too cloſe an imitation of it, is unmuſical, and even grating to the ear.

  O'er hills, o'er dales, o'er crags, o'er rocks, they go.

There is ſomething ſtiff and affected in this line, to which

same manner we may censure as the effect of defective education, or may consider as the style of an uninformed age; but in these likewise, there may be *rusticity* without that *discordance*, to which last, just observation, of whatever kind, can have no affinity.

Harsh diction, occasioned thus at some times by the discordance of words to the sense conveyed in these, is, however, most commonly the effect of ill-constructed periods. We pronounce expression to have this disagreeable peculiarity, when the members of a sentence are broken and disjointed, instead of forming a consistent body; when there is a visible constraint in the choice, as well as disposition of words, and when the conclusion of the period is ungratefully abrupt. Some of

---

which the original by no means corresponds. Again,
Jumping high o'er the shrubs of the rough mound,
Rattle the clattering cars, and the shockt axles bound.
The first of these lines is picturesque, but the last is particularly harsh, and the description is overwrought in it. A writer fond of *conceit* might say here, that the ear of the reader is as much *shocked* by this collection of sounds, as the poet represents the axles of the chariot to have been.

these

these circumstances, it is true, may characterise verbose, as well as concise Composition. A long-winded sentence may be broken, and rendered dissonant more readily than a short one, which, consisting of fewer parts, may be regulated, one may say, with greater facility. But this is the case only when style, though upon the whole deserving the character of *concise*, remote as it must be from the extreme of improper diffusion, is equally so from that of deficiency. It is when a close and contracted manner is studied, that the words, like the jagged points of a rock, unconnected with each other, give the whole Composition this most unfavourable aspect. That harshness in a more particular manner which is occasioned by the abrupt conclusion of periods, is always originally the consequence of studying brevity too universally, and depriving language of its proper ornaments.—The other error into which the affectation of too concise an expression may lead an author, that of *obscurity*, we have considered so fully in other parts of this work, as to supersede

the

the use of an enlargement here*. In order to avoid both the faults we have thus pointed out, as arising from affected brevity, a writer ought to weigh the sentiments or arguments suggested to him together, so as to judge of their comparative energy, and of the words adapted with greatest propriety to each. He who desires to form himself in early life to a nervous style of Composition, will most probably obtain his purpose by taking a thought that hath remarkable energy from some work in which this character predominates; and dropping the words of his original, by endeavouring to express it in his own. When he compares his own attempt with the pattern imitated, he will judge not only of its general conformity to the standard, but of the cause from which a disproportion proceeds. As soon as this is detected, it may be eradicated with facility, not in the single instance alone, but in all cases without exception, where a similar strain of Com-

---

* See sect. ii. and sect. iii. &c. of this volume.

position

position is required to prevail. The observation of this rule tends no doubt to improve, when properly applied, every character of the art. Yet it is peculiarly adapted to that which we have considered in this section, becaufe a nervous manner is of all others the moſt univerſally affected; and at the ſame time in conſequence of the faults allied to it, the moſt difficult to be obtained.

3. The laſt method we ſhall mention of giving this maſterly character to Compoſition, is that of carrying on a *well-conducted climax* in any branch of it whatever. By a *climax*, whether in the language or ſentiment of a performance, we underſtand a gradual progreſſion from the leſs to the more animated, as the objects which the mind contemplates grow in their importance, until the faculty that ſcanned a few general principles with indifference, fixes with cloſe attention on the forcible and intereſting. As every ſubject ought to be treated in this manner, that it may make a ſuitable impreſſion on the power to which it is addreſſed, a ſimilar pro-

procedure in conducting the members of a sentence to its conclusion must naturally be productive of a corresponding effect. This conduct is principally requisite when the motives used to enforce any proposition are placed before the mind in one comprehensive summary; as it is here necessary to concentrate their whole force in *one point*, whose energy may be thus rendered irresistibly penetrating. The effect of such conduct will be felt most powerfully by trying an example.—
" Idemque (says the Roman orator) cum cœlum, terras, maria, rerumque omnium naturam perspexerit, eaque unde generata quo recurrant, quando, quomodo obitura, quid in iis mortale & caducum, quid divinum æternumque sit viderit. *Ipsumque* ea moderantem & regentem pæne prehenderit; *seseque* non unis circumdatum mænibus, popularem alicujus definiti loci; sed *civem totius mundi* quasi *unius urbis* agnoverit:—in *hac magnificentia rerum*; atque in *hoc conspectu & cognitione naturæ*;— DII immortales!—Quam *ipse se* noscet!" De Legib. lib. i.—The gradation here from

from lefs to more interefting circumftances, and the correfponding emphafis communicated to the diction as the author proceeds, can efcape the obfervation of no reader who is able to comprehend an original which any tranflation muft greatly injure.

Thus we have attempted to render the reader acquainted with the proper meaning and fphere of this diftinguifhed character of Compofition, with the caufes that produce, with the *faults* allied to, and with the means of obtaining it. We fhall conclude with obferving, as the refult of all,— that however eminent any characteriftic of the art may be, a writer of good fenfe will take care never to give fuch ftrenuous and clofe attention to that one, as to overlook others of confiderable, perhaps of equal importance. In the purfuit, therefore, of *ftrength*, he will be careful to preferve *harmony* of diction. Thefe, as we have feen in many inftances, are perfectly compatible. The exclufion of the laft from Compofition can be compenfated by the attainment of no excellence whatever.

SEC-.

SECTION VII.

Of correct Composition.

NO branch of the various and comprehensive subject of the present work opens to us a more extensive field of observation, than that with which we here propose to sum up our remarks on the principal characters of the style of Composition. Every writer desires to render his performance correct; and his attention to this circumstance is proportioned to the sollicitude with which he wishes to obtain unallayed approbation. The purpose to which the *critical art* hath been principally subservient in all ages, is that of correcting the faults, of pointing out the defects, and of retrenching the superfluities of inaccurate Composition; by which means, when unwarped by passion or prejudice to selfish gratification, it hath contributed eminently to reform the manners, and promote the happiness of mankind. The truth of this observation we shall illustrate at greater length, when we come to trace the connection of both arts with each other, and to show the tendency of each.

When we consider the most correct performance in this manner, as that in which the nearest approach is made to perfection, the animadversions of some men must appear to be ill-founded, who affirm, that too much attention may be bestowed on this circumstance; that it is often unfavourable to the exertions of genius; and that *exquisite beauty*, though frequently characterising works whose composition is *unequal*, yet is seldom to be met with in those more chastised productions, where the reader finds nothing to censure. We shall here begin with laying before the reader the reasons that are urged on both sides of this question, we shall then endeavour to show what degree of attention this character of the art necessarily claims, and in what cases an author *ought* perhaps to relax in it;—some observations (as usual) on the most proper methods of rendering Composition correct, will conclude the section.

I. It is almost needless to observe here, that the term *correct*, when applied to this art, suggests a negative rather than positive description of any kind. It implies, indeed, the absence of faults, but not the predominance of distinguishing excellence. At the same time this epithet contains nothing in its meaning, either exclusive of such excellence, or incompatible with it. A work eminently characterised by every species of beauty, may be likewise correct. But it is equally true, that a performance in which we find little to censure will always deserve this character, though its excellence may be at most but *secondary*.

It deserves more particular notice, that this phrase, when applied to the various parts, or *members* of Composition (as these may be denominated), hath a more determinate signification than when viewed with relation to the art in general, and such as is positive and direct. Thus by a series of *corrected sentiment*, we understand thoughts that rise naturally out of a subject conveying distinct ideas to the mind; and

and placed in such exact disposition, as that the sense must be injured by altering their arrangement. By a correct *image* in the same manner, we mean one that is appropriated to its original pattern, whose parts correspond exactly to those of this object; to which a retrenchment would give defect, and an addition superfluity. Correct diction is that which being both grammatically accurate, and distinguished by propriety, obtains at once the approbation of the less intelligent, and escapes the censure of the critic.

These remarks on *correct* Composition, lead us naturally to take notice of another circumstance by which it is discriminated from those which have formerly been enumerated. It is, that the present character can be applied more properly than any other to one member or ingredient of the art, though wholly excluded from the rest. We have already seen, that the sublime, and the nervous in particular, never take place unless when there is a concurrence of strong or exalted sentiment, with vigorous, or elevated expression.

This

This holds true likewise of the other criteria we have examined, which communicate a certain *colour*, as it may be called, or peculiarity to language. But no such combination is indispensably requisite to constitute the present character, which may be even *perfect* in its kind, though wholly confined to one object. Thus it will be acknowledged, that the sentimental part of a performance may be correct while the diction is inaccurate; this last chastised again when the former is defective; and an image may be fitted to its original with sufficient accuracy, when both the others lie open to censure. This circumstance, it is, that renders Composition perfectly chastised, so rare and difficult an attainment. Thought and expression forming here no necessary combination, as in the former instances *, cannot be made *equally* correct without the closest attention to both. Yet a want of either, far from being of small consequence, is a capital defect.

From the view we have here exhibited of the present subject, we may, without

---

* See sect. iv. and sect. v. pass.

difficulty, account for that defire which hath obtained among authors in every civilized ftate of fociety, to diftinguifh their performances by the prevalence of this criteria in its utmoft extent; as being fenfible, that though the term *correct* may be applied without impropriety to one in-ingredient of Compofition, exclufively of others; yet that work comes neareft to perfection, in which its influence is moft univerfal.

The reafons, therefore, that are urged for rendering Compofition, in the full meaning of the word, as correct as poffible, are fo obvious and ftriking, as to require no particular enumeration; and far lefs any long enlargement. It is by means of this character alone that a work, in whofe conduct there may be very confiderable ingenuity, affords the mind a rational entertainment, inftead of being laid afide as containing the ebullitions of extravagant imagination, reduced into no form, and exciting the difguft of a fenfible reader, by the frequent violation of decorum and of truth. It is (as we have already feen) the

the peculiar province of underſtanding to
beſtow this laſt heightening on a production *, the maturity, as well as compre-
henſion of which power, is indicated in
proportion as this chaſtiſed manner pre-
vails in one branch of the art, or takes
place equally in all. There are, indeed,
certain deviations from propriety rendered
excuſable by various circumſtances, as the
age in which an author wrote, his time of
life (particularly if poſſeſſed of extenſive
imagination), the nature of his theme, as
demanding materials greatly diverſified;
and, finally, the imperfection of the human mind, extending neceſſarily to its
production of what kind ſoever. This laſt
cauſe muſt be allowed by all to have uni-
verſal influence; and thoſe who have leaſt
of it themſelves, are commonly readieſt to
conſider it as a plea for the greateſt number of defects.

Theſe cauſes, however, operate only
within certain ſpheres, and there are boundaries (if we may thus expreſs it) ſet to

---

* See vol. I. ſect. ii.

their

their dominion, beyond which we permit it not, at any time, to be extended. Thus a writer, whom we know to have lived in a barbarous age, will be readily excufed on this account for falling into a rude and ill-adapted phrafeology. But fhould this be adduced as a plea for that obfcurity which arifeth from perplexed conftruction, or the fimplicity that is violated by inflated defcription, a fenfible critic would reply, that thefe are faults derived, not from the manner of an age, however uncultivated, but from a defect of the author's underftanding. This, he will fay, muft have fuggefted to him if at all adequate to any fphere of Compofition, that perfpicuity requires the members of a fentence to correfpond with each other; and that the fimplicity of language is violated, when it is fwelled out with epithets which injure the fenfe, inftead of adding to its fignificance. The florid, the luxuriant, the digreffive, and even the flowery (of all others the leaft agreeable manner), are likewife excufed as foon as we know the youth of the author; and are contemplated as the firft crop of a young a young tree, whose blossoms, though not hardening into consistence at that time, yet promise a rich crop of fruit when the plant hath arrived at maturity. But as we are induced to overlook the present in this instance, from our expectation of the future, the plea so successfully employed in the cases above-mentioned, would be adduced to no purpose in favour of a frigid, trifling, or insipid production, which affording neither immediate gratification, nor a prospect of future emolument, would be rejected as wholly unworthy our attention. Finally, when we discover great mastery and precision to take place in the general conduct of a work (especially when consisting of very complicated parts), the imperfection of human nature will lead the more discerning part of mankind not only to excuse *great inequalities* in an author's Composition, but even to consider the *less* as compensated fully by the *more material*, when the former is *uniformly* defective and inadequate. But this plea can never be admitted; unless when there is a greater proportion of excellence than of defect,

defect, upon the whole, in a performance. It would otherwise be preferred to no other purpose, than that of exciting indignation.

Correct Composition, therefore, as it renders at all times that work the most valuable of which it is most universally characteristical; so within certain limits no atonement can be made for its deficiency. Those, however, who appear to have examined this matter with close attention are of opinion, that, excellent as it is, the desire of obtaining this character in perfection may be carried so far as to produce bad consequences, and such as are detrimental in particular to authors of the most distinguished eminence *. These represent this task of correcting every inaccuracy, not only as painfully minute, and disagreeeable to a man of genius †, but they
observe,

---

* " Sunt scriptores (says the learned and elegant Erasmus) qui semper aliquid addentes, adimentes, immutantes; & hoc ipso *maxime* peccantes, quia *nihil peccare* conantur." Chil. i. cent. 3.

† Ovid is very honest in making an acknowledgment of this kind.

Seepe

observe, likewise, that there is a certain point beyond which this affectation of chastising every part to the last degree of perfection may injure Composition, but can be of no use to it *. They represent it as an assiduity, by which the vigour and energy of sentiment is drained away,

---

   Sæpe aliquod verbum cupiens mutare, relinquo:
     Judicium vires destituuntque meum.
   Sæpe piget, (quid enim dubitem tibi vera fateri)
     Corrigere, & longi ferre laboris onus:
   Scribentem juvat ipse favor, minuitque laborem,—&c.
   Corrigere at res est tanto magis ardua, quanto
     Magnus Aristarcho major Homerus erat.
   Sic animum lento curarum frigore lædit,
     Ut cupidi si quis fræna retentat equi.—
                        De Pont. lib. Ep. 9.
This, it must be owned, is the language of indolence, but it is an indolence of which *imagination* is the parent. A heavy author would never talk in this manner.

 *. " Cum perfectum absolutumque sit opus, non *splendescit* lima, sed *atteritur*." Plin. Epist. lib. v. Epist. 11. Dionysius censures Isocrates for an attention of this kind. Ισοκρατης πανηγυρικωτερος εςι μαλλον η δικανικωτερος. Εχει δε τον κοσμον μετ' ενεργειας, &c. Ου μεν αγωνιςικος περιγραφων δε την απαγγελιαν τοις περιοδοις ολως μεσοτητα σωφρονιζων λιτοτητι, το δε λιτον εξαιρων. Και αυτε μαλιςα ζηλωτεον την τε των ονοματων συνεχειαν, &c. Τ ΑΡΧΑΙΩΝ ΕΞΕΤΑΣ.

as it were, and tells us, that a work thus elaborately purified, is like a body whose richest blood, and most invigorating juices, are strained off by the physician, who leaves it an heavy, and inanimated carcass *. With regard to the style of Composition, it is said to be rendered, by attempting to deprive it of every superfluity, either so dry and insipid as to be read with listless inattention †; or so scholastic and grammatical as to show that elegance is sacrificed to precision.

But these, though errors that ought to be avoided carefully by those who would be masters of the art, are yet by no means

---

* " Et ipsa emendatio finem habet. Sunt enim qui ad omnia scripta tanquam vitiosa redeant, & quasi nihil fas sit rectum esse quod primum est melius existiment quicquid est aliud, idque faciunt quoties librum in manus resumpserint similes medicis, etiam *integra secantibus*. Accidit itaque ut *cicatricosa* sint, & *exsanguia*, & *cura pejora*." Quint. lib. x.

† " Non minus non servat modum, qui *infra rem*, quam qui supra: qui adstrictius, quam qui effusius dicit. Itaque audis frequenter ut illud immodice & redundanter, ita hoc *jejune* & *infirme*. Alius *excessisse* materiam, alius dicitur *non implesse*. Æque uterque, sed ille *imbecillitati*, hic viribus peccat." Plin. Epist. lib. i. Epist. 20.

the

the principal faults into which authors of the firſt rank are apt to be led, by making too much uſe of the *file* (as it may be termed) in order to give the laſt poliſh to their pieces. It is ſaid, with ſome truth, that though in conſequence of this practice a performance becomes, upon the whole, leſs apt to excite an unpleaſing ſenſation at any time, than when it obtains not; yet it ceaſeth likewiſe, by this means, to excite ſo much admiration.*. In order, therefore, to render a work faultleſs, it is deprived of *capital excellencies*; and a genius which might have gleaned many a wild, though exquiſite beauty, had it been

---

* Shall I offend any *rational* admirer of Pope (ſays a critic well qualified to judge of his ſubject) by remarking that ſome juvenile deſcriptive poems of Milton (l'Allegro, Il Penſeroſo, and Ode on the Nativity) as well as his Latin elegies, are of a ſtrain far more exalted than any the former author can boaſt. Let me add at the ſame time, what juſtice obliges me to add, that they are far more *incorrect*. For in the very Ode before us (that on the Nativity) occur one or two paſſages, that are puerile and affected to a degree not to be paralleled in the *purer*, but *leſs elevated* compoſitions of Pope. Eſſay on the Writings and Genius of Pope, p. 40.

left

left to expatiate on the common of nature, yet like a bird taken from this field, and confined within a circumscribed and scanty space, it ranges among a few objects, instead of viewing an exhaustless variety, and finds its wings every moment repelled by the bars of its dungeon. It is worth while to enquire what truth there is in this observation, as this will introduce a branch of our subject not yet touched upon, how far the desire of rendering their performances *correct* ought to operate on writers of exalted genius.

This great and extraordinary quality, constituted by the union of the superior faculties in vigorous exertion, is yet, no doubt, distinguished principally by strokes derived from imagination. On this account it is, that as the native bias of this power directs it to form elevated, forcible, picturesque, or beautiful imitations of the objects that pass before it, we denominate the genius of the writer to be sublime, vigorous, animated, or elegant. The inventive faculty, therefore, in general determines our application of the word Genius
to

to any mind; while the character belonging to it is fixed by that modification which we perceive to take place. From thefe principles it naturally follows, that the higheft walk of genius is that in which imagination makes the greateft and moft aftonifhing exertions. But in what circumftances are thefe exertions made? Is it not neceffary for this purpofe, that the power above mentioned fhould be permitted to take cognizance of a feries of objects, at once great and diverfified; and that a field, proportioned to this diverfity, fhould be opened for its range, as they will thus be obferved to the greateft advantage?

That both ought to take place here will not be difputed. It remains, therefore, that we enquire by what means the range of imagination is moft contracted, and the feweft objects prefented to its cognizance. Both thefe are confequences of attending clofely to the circumftance of *ftrict propriety* in every idea, and of beftowing on it not the richeft colouring, but fuch as is most decent and suitable. We do not deny that this choice is made by the understanding, and that whatever receives its approbation, will be considered as the fittest and least exceptionable. We mean only to observe, that in consequence of the severe investigation carried on by this faculty, many objects will be rejected as unfit, which might have pleased by being decorated with certain admirable graces; and what these obtain by this intervention in point of accuracy, they lose in wildness, variety, and grandeur. This, upon reflection, will appear not to be an adventitious but necessary effect, arising from the ends which the powers here mentioned propose separately to bring about, fancy attracted always by *beauty*, and judgment directed by *propriety*. These ought, no doubt, to be generally united in ordinary cases. Elegance is improved by regularity; but the wild and luxuriant require it to be violated. We are pleased when cultivated inclosures, laid out with all the improvements of art, terminate with the prospect

of

of broken rocks, immense mountains, or stupendous precipices; in the same manner as we prefer the irregular grandeur of a Gothic pile, to the most perfect plan of modern architecture, executed with so much judgment as to present few, or no objects, that require to be rectified. The protuberances in both are violations of *correct design.* But they are such violations as no man, possessed of the least perception of beauty, would wish to remove. There is a grandeur in the appearance of certain objects, which compensates in the estimation of every beholder for the defect of regularity. Imagination dwells upon this circumstance with intense enjoyment; and reason *stands aside,* as it were, while the mind is entranced with its idea, and dasheth not its pleasure by the thought of disproportion.

These remarks bear a strict and obvious application to the present subject. In the sphere of philosophy, considered as of the most extensive import, and in every province that is occupied principally by the under-

understanding, the first thing to be considered is correctness of disposition. A writer can only be said to carry his attention to an extreme in this point, when he extends it to minute circumstances; or by re-touching every part with unremitting assiduity, deprives his work of vigour and character. The same observation may be made on historical Composition, and on that of eloquence (as we shall show afterwards), when in the simple proof of any proposition the orator neither speaks to the imagination, nor toucheth the heart. But when we consider the more peculiar department of exalted genius in Composition, the sublime, and pathetic, it must be acknowledged, that not only are the capital beauties of these such as imagination strikes out at once in the fervor of abstracted contemplation, but when we attempt to describe the circle within which she ought to be confined, her most shining attractions are no longer perceivable, and even that character which the *close* superintendence of judgment renders regular and

and confiftent, becomes at the fame time languid and uninterefting *.

What

---

* The character of Cato, in the celebrated tragedy of that name, affords a pregnant example to the prefent purpofe. That this character is juft, and rendered confiftent by the moft judicious conduct, will admit of as little difpute as that the Hamlet of Shakefpeare is frequently irregular and offenfive. The former (which Voltaire affirms to be the greateft character that ever was brought upon any ftage, Lettr. fur le Traged.) is uniformly great, and " nothing is uttered " by Cato (as a contemporary critic juftly obferves) " but what is worthy of the beft of men." Guard. Numb. 33. Hamlet, on the contrary, fcruples to kill the king of Denmark at his prayers left he fhould go to heaven, but propofeth to take him in the commiffion of fome deed, which may make his foul " as damn'd and black as hell whereto it goes." Cato utters no fentiment but fuch as reafon approves, and is confiftent with the dignity of his rank and character. Hamlet, giving a loofe to the wildeft imagination, afks his friend, " why we may not trace the duft of " Alexander till we find it ftopping a bung hole." Act v. fcene 1. Yet with all this irregularity in the latter, Hamlet is, upon the whole, not only an amiable, but an exalted character. He holds (if we may thus exprefs it) the *keys of the human heart*, from which he calls out alternately, love, pity, terror, indignation, grief, amazement, horror, and anguifh; while the Roman, with all his perfections, is cold and uninterefting. We admire his virtues, as we may do thofe of a deceafed friend;—but the uniformity of thefe is fuch

What (it may here be asked) is the tendency of these observations? Is it the author's

such as that any reader may guess at the general tenor of his discourse when he knows his situation. He cannot, therefore, be much moved by it. Whence does this striking difference take its rise? Without ascribing it to a disparity of genius betwixt two writers, who both do honour to their country, we may observe, that the author of Cato appears to have been too intent upon rendering his principal character *perfect*, to make it deeply interesting. Such a personage is indeed an object of admiration, whose original is coldly contemplated at a distance; but it can never be so of *love*, which is only excited when virtues, weaknesses, foibles, and blemishes, are blended so happily into one piece as to present a mind similar in some respects to our own. In order to obtain this last end, the wild sallies of imagination must be often admitted into the most dignified species of Composition, whereas the *design* of the former is *incorrect* when these are not wholly excluded Shakespeare, therefore, born with an unbounded reach of imagination, lived in an age when he was at liberty to indulge it. Hence his Falstaff, Hamlet, Prospero, Orlando, and many other persons, are such just pictures of human nature, represented in *every sphere* of life, that the fable of Narcissus may here be said to be realized; and while we are enchanted with this various assemblage, the poet's address to him may be applied with strict propriety to us in many cases,

Ista repercussæ quam cernis imaginis umbra est.

and again,

—— tecum

thor's intention to represent *design* as inconsistent with *any degree* of excellence, and the most *careless* writers as the most successful?—As it cannot be supposed, that any author will attempt to support either of these assertions, we shall now

―――― tecum venitque, manetque
Tecum discedet, si tu discedere possis.

But Addison, on the other hand, flourished at a time when the principal excellence of Composition was judged to be the *chastised* manner we are here considering; and, in truth, no author ever obtained it more thoroughly than he. But fettered in this pursuit by the laws of criticism, while his eye was fixed on *propriety*, it lost sight of *nature*; and that imagination which displays such *enchanting luxuriance* in his *prose compositions*, is rendered unanimated in its *proper province* by castigation. Had Shakespeare himself flourished in the age of Addison, how many of his most exquisite beauties must have been sacrificed to the preservation of *certain unities* which he hath notoriously violated; of rules, which a great genius can neither follow without losing its claim to originality, nor break through without incurring the censure of little minds unable to comprehend his motives! Even the excellencies of this admirable writer, in such a situation, would have appeared like flowers that languish on the parterre when transplanted from their native soil, fitted only to show, by displaying some charms in the *garden of art*, with what superior beauty they would have attracted every eye in the *wilderness* of nature.

proceed to enquire how far correct Composition ought to be studied in scientifical research, and in what degree it should characterise the highest exertion of elevated genius. This is a subject which we have not yet entered upon, and which will serve, when examined in its full extent, to complete the view we proposed to take of the characters of Composition.

II. As we have already seen, that to render any branch of the art here examined correct, is the province of understanding, we may naturally conclude, that this signature will prevail principally in such spheres as the power above-mentioned engrosseth most to itself, and in which it is least embarrassed by the interposition of any other. Whatever hath a tendency to hurry the mind in any of its pursuits, by throwing the man off his guard, necessarily imparts confusion to his ideas, and inaccuracy to his manner of expressing them. This effect ariseth most commonly from some improper influence, exerted either by the imagination, or the passions. The first of these renders thoughts diffused

when

when they ought to ſtand cloſely together, or ornamented when ſimplicity is requiſite. The latter not only fruſtrate, but pervert reaſon to wrong purpoſes, and ſtamp upon the Compoſition of a writer, the certain marks of their own irregularity. We may, therefore, ſay with Cæſar, in the celebrated oration above referred to *.— " Omnes homines qui de *rebus dubiis* conſultant, ab odio, ira, amicitia, atque miſericordia vacuos eſſe debent. Haud facile animus *verum providet* ubi *illa* officiunt."

Of the inequality occaſioned by either of theſe cauſes, the Compoſition of philoſophy and hiſtory, ought to be ſo much corrected as to exhibit the feweſt poſſible examples. An author ought likewiſe, in either of theſe provinces, to give the cloſeſt attention to the juſt connection and diſpoſition of his ſentiments, that theſe may follow each other naturally, and may form altogether a body made up of parts that are mutually proportioned. With regard

---

* See ſect. iv. of book II.

to those enlargements on every topic, which will occur to the mind upon reflection, when its principal work is over, and those little alterations which are made with the view of superseding some frivolous objection, or of rendering the import of some thought more perspicuous, there is no end of such indulgence as this, which after all must fail of answering any purpose. Far from rendering sentiments unexceptionable, this restless assiduity serves only to throw an air of perplexity and embarrassment over a performance, and the writer can scarce expect his reader to be pleased, when he appears incapable of being so himself. An understanding, whose perceptions of truth or falshood are originally clear, will place them upon making one comprehensive examination in the most suitable points of view. But when the case is different, its utmost repeated efforts may render the perplexity still greater, but will never remove it.

We do not mean here to affirm, as may at first be supposed, that after having once methodised and digested his thoughts, an author

author should not take any subsequent view of these. He only can be said to have made an examination sufficiently comprehensive, who not only endeavours to turn a thought on all sides in his own mind, so as to judge of its truth, and of the exceptions to which it lies open; but who has, at the same time, a dispassionate temper which fits him for hearing the judgment of others, and who readily submits to such animadversions as his own reason, uninfluenced by any selfish motive, approves as well-founded. There is, we may observe in general, no surer evidence of great intellectual debility, than the desire which some men discover, not merely to defend their errors, when candidly pointed out, against the exceptions of others, but even, if possible, to hide these from themselves. A performance we may safely pronounce, whatever excellence it may possess, must fail of being correct, as long as its author is actuated by this principle; since, besides that, an impartial critic can judge much more properly of the elucidation which certain points may require in order

order to produce their effect, than the writer himself, to whom these are familiar; such conduct, even supposing the author's understanding to be *perfect*.(if such a supposition can be made without a solecism in this case), must still be exceptionable, while he addresseth himself to those whose judgment is fallible and uncertain. Upon the whole, therefore, the distinct nature of ideas, as having no coincidence; their proper selection, as means to promote an ultimate purpose; their order, as mutually supporting each other; and their truth, as evinced against material objections;—these are points of essential consequence, to which, therefore, great attention ought to be given, in order to render the sentiment of Composition properly correct. But when the writer hath availed himself of the resources above-mentioned, so as to be satisfied of these capital circumstances, a minute investigation carried on into every little error which rigid criticism may detect, is an endless labour at the same time that it is of no utility, because not only will one man judge that to be well explained,

explained, which another may deem faulty; or that to be perfectly intelligible, which another may have charged with obscurity; but even the same person will be found to vary at different times in his judgment of such points; and that from causes whose influence is unavoidable and universal.

The same finical attention to exactness which is thus detrimental to philosophical sentiment, will be equally so to the language that conveys it. It is when words are moulded into a certain form with much labour, that Composition acquires a stiffness, which we express by saying, that such diction *smells of the lamp*, i. e. bears the marks of having been wrought up with much toil and difficulty. Art (it is universally acknowledged) makes the highest effort we expect from her when she disappears in an imitation, so as to leave no traces by which her step may be marked. It is a mistake to suppose that this apparent want of design (as it may be termed), is obtained by much thought, and costs the writer many elaborate exertions.

ertions. In fact, it is partly the effect of that easy freedom with which the intellectual powers act, when unrestrained in their exercise, by too close an attention to rules; and partly, of being early accustomed to the imitation of some model in which this character is conspicuous. The last cause, in particular, operates much more powerfully than we are apt at first view to suppose. That general similarity which we observe in the diction even of the most approved contemporary authors, and which marks the productions of an age, as more or less conformable to a certain standard, hath its origin in the imitation here referred to. We have already considered this subject at some length *. It is to the present purpose only to observe, that too much attention to make the style, especially of philosophical or historical Composition, correct, by attempting to render every word almost distinguished by significance, and every period by being

---

* See sect. iv.

elaborately

elaborately rounded, introduceth as naturally that constraint into expression, which is incompatible with correctness, as the desire to please, when too remarkably predominant, taints the manners with aukwardness and reserve.

The expression of a performance is, upon the whole, sufficiently correct, when the character, whatever it may be that is required to predominate, is well supported, and the fault most nearly allied to it is either wholly avoided, or so rarely and inconsiderably permitted to appear, as will give no offence to those who are most susceptible of being impressed by it. Thus simplicity, a character required to distinguish every species of Composition, ought always to be preserved distinct from a certain plain and insipid uniformity of diction *; just perspicuity from finical exactness †; elegance demanding ease and harmony, from quaintness and affected brilliance, inconsistent with both ‡; sublimity

---

* Sect. ii.　† Sect. iii.　‡ Sect. iv.

from bombaſt *; and energy from harſhneſs, diffuſion, and obſcurity †. We have endeavoured to ſhow, in other parts of this work, by what means this important purpoſe may be moſt probably, and completely effectuated, in each of theſe inſtances. The faults here mentioned are ſuch, as when taking place, univerſally disfigure Compoſition, and deſtroy, in a great meaſure, the effect which it is propoſed principally to bring about in any branch of it. On this account they ought to be avoided by every writer; for which end, we have placed both the excellence, and the error reſembling it, in one point of view before the reader, and have illuſtrated each by ſeparate examples, that having both before him, he may know, as nearly as poſſible, at what point the former obtains in perfection, and when by attempting to purſue it too far he will fall into the laſt.

2. It is a remark which every man of letters hath met with, both in books, and

---
* Sect. v.   † Sect. vi.

Observations on Composition. 305

in converfation, that rules in general are unfavourable to the exertions of a great imagination *; that on this account, the works upon which men in all ages have dwelt with the higheft admiration, are fuch as either preceded the exiftence of critical inquifition, or cannot yet ftand the teft of its rigid inveftigation; and that in general, the pieces rendered by fevere attention moft exactly conformed to a certain ftandard, are thofe which exhibit the feweft examples of confummate excellence †.

But

---

* Some of the ancients have for this purpofe given fuch definitions of poetry, as muft exclude the application of rules to the art. Thus Plato terms it, Ενθεια Δυναμις; & ΜΙΜΗΣΙΣ. A Latin critic expreffeth himfelf ftill more particularly. " Per ambages, Deorumque minifteria, & fabulofum fententiarum tormentum præcipitandus eft liber fpiritus ut potius furentis animi vaticinatio adpareat, quam religiofæ orationis fub teftibus fides," fays Petronius Arbiter, fpeaking of the difference betwixt poetic and hiftorical narration. This, however, is carrying the matter too far. But the examination of both belongs to another part of this work.

† As a confirmation of this remark it may be obferved, that the greateft genuifes have failed moft confpicuoufly when they have attempted to render thofe

Vol. II.   X   pieces

But these general observations, however true, answer no purpose of importance, as long as we do not ascertain the influence which this character ought to exert in the highest, as well as in the less difficult departments of genius; as it is certain that a performance of any kind, in which no attention is paid to it, must present such a jumble of incoherent ideas, as no rational mind can contemplate with satisfaction.— It may, therefore, be proper here, to

---

pieces correct which attracted admiration in their original form. Bayle has preserved a curious anecdote to this purpose of Tasso, which accounts for the difference betwixt his Gierusalemme Liberata, and Conquistata, at least in some measure. In an attempt to correct the last (improperly conducted it should appear) he cancelled some of the greatest beauties, and substituted in their place, others that are unintelligible. " A quali tutti (says the Italian critic, after having enlarged on the former) gratissimi e giocondissimi auvenimente sustituisse il Tasso cose tali che se con semplice intelligenza debbono prenderfi, sono si frivole, che niente piu, e se ci e dentro qualche miftero, egli ci e involto con tante ambagi ch'a sottrarnelo non basterebbe l'isteflo Edippo." Diction. Crit. &c. Art. RONSARD. The predecessors of this illustrious writer in the same high department of genius, avoid a censure of this kind, by having attempted no such emendations.

enter

enter into this subject a little more particularly.

The laws of criticism considered as sanctions established by the understanding, for the purpose of rendering any species of Composition a proper vehicle, either of emolument or entertainment, various as these are, may yet be comprehended under the three following heads.—They are either of that kind whose obligation is at all times indispensable, and which cannot be violated without defeating the ultimate purpose of the art:—or of such a nature, as though always approved by reason, when justly observed, may yet be dispensed with upon some occasions that justify the neglect:—or, lastly, these consist of certain incidental circumstances tagged to the former which are essential, deriving their origin from accident, and established principally by use.

Under the first head we may compreprehend the general method or plan upon which any piece is laid out, whether obvious or concealed; the tendency of its parts to promote an ultimate end; the union of these into one body, so as to render it coherent and proportioned; a depth, or strength of conception, adapted to the subject; and, finally, a just correspondence of language to the objects, of whatever kind, that are set before the mind. These are principles which it requires no great attention to convince us, adhere to the very essence of Composition, and cannot be dispensed with *without* rendering any performance capitally **defective**. As, therefore, the human mind hath at all times considered these as fundamental rules, which must be observed in every instance, the decisions of criticism when they are violated, however severe, are yet rational, and proportioned to the breach of an indispensible requisition.

But when so much attention is bestowed on the radical characters here enumerated, as that reason approves of them upon the whole, as being well preserved; there are other points in judging of which this faculty relaxeth of its severity, and though

always

always satisfied when these are closely adhered to, yet judgeth their neglect upon some occasions to be compensated by the attainment of a noble end. We may comprise in this class, the use of episodes, and digressive circumstances, the connection of which with the principal subject, may be somewhat remote; the introduction of images not appropriated with perfect accuracy to their originals; thoughts distinguished by a certain boldness, suited rather to the character of the speaker than to the occasion, and principally thrown out to set the former in some new point of view; illustrations that are beautiful rather as distinct pictures, than as strictly conformed to a model; and, finally, flights of imagination wholly excentric, and excusable only on account of their wildness or sublimity. In these cases, as it is necessary to deviate from strict propriety in order to raise admiration, we judge that a nobler purpose is obtained by the breach of an established law, than could have resulted from a rigid adherence to it; and therefore ceafe to apply it where it muft be deficient.

Laftly, we may regard as circumftances wholly incidental, derived from accident, and eftablifhed by cuftom, fuch rules as regard the divifion of dramatic pieces into a particular number of acts; the opening of an epic poem in the middle of the action which it celebrates; an attempt to comprife it likewife within a certain determinate number of books, as if the fpirit of the great mafters of the epopœa would be transfufed into him who *touched the fkirt of their garments*. A fervile adherence to the unities of the drama, belongs likewife to this clafs of laws, confecrated by ufe, rather than approved by the reafon of mankind; as the lofs of one ftroke of nature and paffion, excluded from a performance in confequence of fuch an adherence, and far more the abfence of many of thefe left out by this practice, will not be thought by any reader of difcernment, to be compenfated by the ftricteft obfervation of the mechanifm of the drama,

that

that can be supposed to take place in any production *.

From this general division of the rules which criticism hath established for the conduct of Composition, it will be readily concluded, that the two last classes are the only ones in which genius may meet with a considerable share of indulgence. The principles laid down under the first head, are altogether out of the question.—But here I am aware, that a critical inquisitor may strenuously urge a very plausible objection.—" The laws, he may say, by
" which every species of Composition
" ought to be tried, are ordained like those
" of civil government in some sense, to

---

* Some of the last-mentioned circumstances (it may be said) ought not to be included in an enumeration of established rules in the province of criticism, but are rather arbitrary modes derived from imitation. They are here, however, considered as rules, because a performance would be excepted against in which the least of them (that only excluded, which regards the *number* of books in an epic poem) was omitted; and as *established* rules, because with whatever truth reason may exclaim against their observance in particular instances, custom hath rendered it expedient to carry them most commonly into practice.

" main-

"maintain order in their departments, and to substitute in place of a wild and faulty exuberance, such judicious conduct as a sensible mind will ever view with approbation. So intimately are these connected with each other, that the least innovation ought to be considered as a precedent leading by natural steps to the greatest. Though, therefore, the highest branches of Composition may lose some advantages by being thus rigidly conformed to established laws, yet it ought to be remembered, that when this conformity is disregarded, confusion must immediately take place of regularity, and that at worst, if the mind is deprived of pleasure in some instances when certain rules are adhered to, it meets with fewer objects to censure than when they are violated."

We might reply in general to this series of observation, that it would have had much more force at any less enlightened period than the present, when men were not thoroughly acquainted with the tests

Observations on Composition. 313

by which criticism tries every object; because the frequent violation of her laws might then have been productive of consequences, which now, when these are universally known, there is less reason to apprehend. We will allow, however, so much weight to the objection, as that in order to obviate it properly the reasons ought to be assigned for which a licence is sometimes granted of deviating from received principles; the cases to be specified with precision in which this licence may take place; and the bounds to be assigned with accuracy, beyond which it ought never to be extended. Let us consider each of these in its place.

1. We have already laid down in this section, the reasons which make it necessary to grant an indulgence to writers of exalted genius, when we find them assuming liberties in the two last mentioned departments of the laws of criticism, which would be justly censured in those of an inferior class. It is, therefore, needless to dwell on this branch of the subject at present. We may only add to our enumera-

tion

tion of these causes, a remark that may reconcile even the most rigid defender of critical despotism to the infringement of its rules upon some occasions;—viz. that the discerning faculty after all is the ultimate judge to which an appeal is made concerning this infringement, as justified or not by the purpose to be obtained by it. Every deviation of this kind is considered as hazardous. Curiosity is excited to trace out its effect: and even when sallies of imagination the most excentric, bewilder the mind for some time in its pursuit, the whole terminates at last in this point, whether these, when viewed as irregularities in the methodised order of Composition, are real violations of an essential law; or whether they are breaches of some subordinate nature, whose inequality may be amply compensated by the pleasure of which they are productive. Of this matter, the discerning faculty must finally take cognizance. Of the superior powers, by whose union it is constituted, imagination impresseth the idea in all its strength upon the mind, and reason enables it to judge

in

in what respects it is, or is not, conformed to the laws of criticism.

2. With regard to the particular cases in which the neglect of correct Composition may be justified, we have likewise mentioned, in general, the principal of these in the enumeration above referred to. It is a rule with which we expect writers of genius to comply, particularly in the higher spheres of its exercise, that the episodes, or digressive parts of a performance, should be wrought in such a manner into the body of the piece, as to complete, instead of disfiguring its proportion; and should appear like rays of light, which, though diverging at first in various directions from their centre, yet may be made to terminate in one point, and co-operate in the accomplishment of a general end. On this account, an author ought in most cases to be cautious, both of deviating too often from his principal subject *, and of striking too far into the

---

* " Les Tragedies les plus defectueuses sont celles dont les episodes n'ont point de liaison ensemble;
Aristote

the paths that lead from it, left he break that union of parts in which excellence confifts; and bewilder at the fame time both his reader and himfelf *.—But this rule is not without exception. There are circumftances apparently remote, and even foreign to the point in view, that yet compenfate at laft for having thrown it for a time out of the reader's fight, by that light which they are brought to beftow upon it in the end, as well as by the peculiar beauties which thefe may poffefs when contemplated as diftinct pieces. A great genius far from being expofed to cenfure on account of fuch an introduction of digreffive circumftances, will be judged on the contrary, to have difplayed confummate maftery by the manner in which

---

Ariftote les nomme *epifodiques* c'eft a dire furabondantes en epifodes, parce que ces moindres epifodes ne peuvent en compofer un feul; mais demeurent neceffairement en cette pluralité vicieufe." Boffu du Poëme Epique, liv. ii. chap. 2.

* " Les actions les plus fimples, & les moins intriguées, etoient le plus fujettes a cette irregularité, parce qu'ayant moins d'incidens, & moins de parties que les autres, elles fourniffent auffi moins de matieres," &c. Id. ibid.

they

they are made to fall at laſt into his ſubject, as harmony will thus appear to ariſe from the diſpoſition of materials ſo complicated as an inferior hand muſt have involved in confuſion *. The law demanding exact proportion to be accurately preſerved in every caſe, is, no doubt, after all violated in ſuch inſtances; but in this violation we obſerve a degree of excellence diſplayed which a tame, though faultleſs compliance with the rule, muſt have effectually ſuperſeded.

When again, we pronounce either a particular thought, or a certain train of ſentiment to be remarkably *bold*, the idea of *temerity* enters in ſome degree into our eſtimation; and whatever bears the marks of this character excludes that of correctneſs. But a diſcerning critic will weigh

---

* We have conſidered this ſubject at ſo much length in a former eſſay, and have endeavoured to illuſtrate our remarks ſo particularly to the caſe of Pindar, whoſe digreſſions are bolder and more excentric than thoſe of any other author; that we beg leave to refer to that piece the reader whom curioſity may prompt to ſee the obſervations in the text exemplified. Eſſ. on Lyr. Poet. let. ii. p. 95 to 98.

one circumstance against another, in order to know how far an author is, on this account, an object of admiration or censure; and will consider, that what may be unappropriated to the occasion, may yet have peculiar merit, as being adapted to the character of the speaker in some branches of Composition*; as in others, the same thoughts that strongly evince the *genius of the writer*, contain an impeachment on the *prudence*, or even *virtue of the man*. As critics, however, these objects not only obtain our forgiveness, on account of the qualities which we suppose to have given rise to them, but even command involuntary admiration.

This is the case, likewise, with those irregular sallies of imagination which appear to have been thrown out, as it were, at random, rather as if the writer had been impelled by an enthusiastic impulse, to break into some abrupt apostrophe, than

---

* Let the candid, and discerning, apply this remark to the buffooneries (as they are termed) by many of the persons introduced into Shakespeare's plays, particularly in the comic parts.

like

like him, who, with both the superior faculties acting in just combination, should conduct a regulated process to a period. A piece, in which many strokes of this kind were to be met with, it is confessed might with justice be censured as incorrect by *the judicious*; but would it, therefore, cease to be admired as exquisitely beautiful by the *discerning* critic?—By the former, upon being tried by a certain standard, these might be condemned as effusions unconnected with the subject, and forming excrescencies that disfigure its symmetry:—by the latter, they would be prized as imitations of nature, the wildness or magnificence of whose works compensate, in numberless instances, for an apparent irregularity of disposition *.—Thus, therefore, in each of the cases mentioned

---

* The highest productions of genius, and those in which the mind makes the most astonishing efforts, are the works where we will meet with examples of the kind here enumerated. A selection of these here, would have answered little other purpose than that of protracting the work. To a penetrating judge such beauties need not be pointed out, and by readers of another cast, they would not be comprehended.

here,

here, we permit strokes to be thrown into Composition that render it incorrect when strictly examined, not merely without censuring these on this account, but even with pleasure, when we reflect that a noble purpose hath been effectuated in consequence of an exertion not otherwise to be allowed.

3. But is not (it will be said) the method *essentially* necessary, as we have already shown, to be observed in every species of the art, broke in upon when such unlicensed freedoms are taken at any time, and are justified as sources of happiness, rather than overlooked as the consequences of inadvertency? Or admitting that, in some few cases, the delight with which a masterly stroke is contemplated may atone for it as the violation of a rule, ought not *some bound* to be fixed, beyond which no acquisition, however eminent, can make up for a temerity inexcusable, as it indicates a defect of understanding? This last requisition is unquestionably reasonable; and in order to answer it as nearly as possible, we shall here make a few observations.

1. The

1. The term *incorrect*, when applied to any branch of the art here treated of, in which we might meet with such strokes as have been enumerated, would characterise it, not as a work in whose conduct no regard was paid to an arrangement that is indispensably requisite; but merely as containing certain irregularities, which, without breaking the general unity of design, are yet inconsistent with perfect accuracy; and might be deemed superfluities. That order in which objects ought at all times to be presented to the mind, is then only essentially violated, when an undue weight appears to be laid upon the less, which thus take place of the more important; or when circumstances wholly foreign to the principal point are introduced, and are pursued without any fixed intention. In these cases, instead of a methodised series, we meet with a promiscuous jumble of discordant ideas, which the mind can neither contemplate with pleasure nor information. In whatever instances, therefore, we observe either of these criteria universally to predominate,

no reader can be at a loss to pronounce a suitable decision.—But it is evident, that the deviations from exact disposition, which we have represented here as justifiable on some occasions, fall not under either of these heads. For it cannot, surely, be said, that objects comparatively insignificant, are obtruded upon the reader in place of such as have importance, when it is only in consequence of the high estimation of these, that their introduction is rendered excusable. Instead, on the other hand, of circumstances promiscuously assembled, and pursued without any fixed intention, the licence here vindicated is principally that which throws a strong light upon some capital object; and though a large compass may be taken in order to effectuate this purpose, yet at last impresseth it with an energy which it could not otherwise have acquired.

2. As those liberties in Composition, whose use we endeavour to vindicate, are such as make no *real* encroachment upon the order established in every species of it, so they can likewise occur but rarely in

any

any cafe, and are confined moſt commonly (though not indeed always) to a particular branch of the art. Exuberant imagery, daring appeals, abrupt tranſitions, bold ſentiments, and wild ſallies of imagination, are not often to be met with in the peruſal of any writings, and are highly characteriſtical of the higher ſpecies of poetry. Bold and new thoughts often thrown out without methodical accuracy, will, no doubt, ſometimes point out the track of philoſophical diſcernment, even in that ſphere where correctneſs ought to be the diſtinguiſhing character. But as it is the author's buſineſs here not to *paint*, but to *prove the truth* of certain propoſitions; not to dazzle the mind with novelty, but to convey ſatisfactory information to the underſtanding; whatever tends to perplex the reader's attention, by withdrawing it from the principal point, or to render his view inadequate by the interruption of unexpected tranſition, ought to be carefully avoided, as inaccuracies which disfigure his work, and which are not to be compenſated by any external advantages whatever.

ever. Freedom of sentiment he may indeed indulge, and audacity, when these are conformed to the standard of truth, will serve to render their impression stronger and more permanent. But his deviations (if at all allowable) ought to be short, even though obviously growing, as it were, out of the subject; his illustrations calculated rather to show truth in a *clear*, than in animated colours; and when he riseth to the sublime of sentiment, the admiration of his readers must be excited, not by the display of the writer's imagination, but by the extent and compass of his judgment, or discernment.

History, whose Composition is much more diversified than that of philosophy, admits but rarely of the licenses above enumerated, and would lose its principal excellence, considered as the vehicle of facts related with impartial accuracy, by their introduction. The pen of an historian must, no doubt, be guided by the events of which he treats; and his diction may with propriety be not only forcible, but highly figured, when the stronger passions

sions are naturally awakened by the detail of great or interesting transactions *. It is, however, at all times incumbent upon him to avoid peculiarity, which will always expose his candour to suspicion; and such liberties in particular, as in other spheres of Composition are viewed with an astonishment which suspends censure, would in this be deemed indications of undue partiality, or of an imagination not properly temperated by the controul of understanding. From both these sciences the wild and exuberant, as deriving their effect wholly from the fervor of irregular imagination, must be wholly excluded at all times without exception.

---

* " Narrat sane illa, narrat & hæc (says a celebrated ancient, speaking of the difference betwixt eloquence and history); sed illi omnia splendida, recondita, excelsa conveniunt. Hanc, (orationem) sæpius ossa, musculi, nervi, illam (historiam) tori quidam & quasi jubæ decent. Hæc vel maxime vi, amaritudine, instantia. Illa tractu, & suavitate, atque etiam dulcedine placet. Postremo alia verba, alius sonus, alia constructio. Nam plurimum refert, ut Thucydides ait, KTHMA sit an ΑΓΩΝΙΣΜΑ quorum alterum oratio, alterum historia est." Plin. Epist. lib. v. epist. 8.

It is, therefore, almoſt only in the two higher ſpheres of eloquence and poetry, that the delight with which certain ſtrokes are contemplated by ſuch readers as are capable of feeling their force, is judged fully to compenſate for that appearance of incorrectneſs which their admiſſion naturally gives to Compoſition. With regard to the rhetorical art, the leaſt reflection will convince us, that with whatever preciſion its general laws may be determined, much greater latitude may be taken in this ſphere preſenting an exhauſtleſs variety of ſubjects, than in the more regulated provinces of philoſophy and hiſtory. In theſe laſt, the proceſs of argument carried on from leſs to more obvious truths, or the detail of tranſactions following each other in a certain natural and eſtabliſhed order, forbid the uſe of bold deviations in almoſt any caſe; becauſe the powers which it is moſt commonly propoſed to impreſs by means of theſe, are weakly if at all excited in the laſt mentioned departments. Hiſtory, indeed, ſometimes addreſſeth herſelf to the paſſions, and even adopts, as we have ſeen, the

the glowing idioms of imagination. But what in her sphere is only a secondary purpose, becomes a principal one in that of the orator; and though it is by different exertions of the intellectual powers that he kindles the imagination, and speaks to the heart (which are therefore considered as distinct provinces of the art), yet the boldest images of the former are introduced so naturally into this last address, that we not only excuse these, but are even led to contemplate them with admiration *.

It

---

* Was it necessary to establish the truth of this observation by examples, we might adduce many from the highest standards of eloquence, both ancient and modern. One, because it is remarkably striking, the reader will peruse with particular pleasure. It is taken from a masterly discourse of Dr. Fordyce, on the Folly and Infamy of Unlawful Pleasure. In this description of the death of an abandoned libertine, wrought up with strokes that are worthy of Demosthenes, he hath contrived to heighten the *pathos* of the scene by admitting into it one of the most picturesque images ever seized by a sublime imagination.—" The dread-
" ful alternative (says he) entirely misgives him. He
" meditates the *devouring abyss of eternity!*—He *recoils*
" as he *eyes* it!"—There is something (if we may thus
express

It ought likewife to be obferved, that eloquence not only includes (as we fhall fhow more particularly afterwards) both the

exprefs it) folemn, and awfully pathetic in this defcription, arifing from the *colour* that imagination cafts on it, which without this heightening could never have taken place. It is no doubt true, in general, that the heart is moft powerfully impreffed when a few circumftances are expreffed in plain, but forcible words, and are put together in fuch a manner as to form a climax. The appeals likewife, by which it is moft deeply penetrated, require to be conveyed in few and unornamented expreffions. The exclamation of Gracchus, which Cicero tells us drew tears from every hearer, is a mafter-piece of this laft kind. " Quo me mifer conferam? (faid he foon after the death of his brother) quo vertam?—In Capitoliumne?—At fratris fanguine redundat.—An domum? Ibi confpicere matrem miferam, lamentantemque & abjectam." De Orat. lib. iii. c. 55. When the real or fuppofed fufferer fpeaks in the firft perfon, it is only by fuch plain, though animated expoftulations as thefe, that a powerful impreffion can be made upon the heart. It is feldom, indeed, that high colouring ought to be admitted into the pathetic part of a difcourfe, unlefs when narration is employed by fome third perfon to accomplifh this purpofe. But genius claims as its privilege, an exemption from thefe rules. It is one of the fignatures of this great character to ftrike out light from objects that are commonly deemed leaft capable of producing it; and even the *inroads* that are made by an exuberant imagination, properly regulated

into

the philosophical and historical characters, by uniting in its comprehensive sphere the didactic with the narrative manner; but even its principal ends, that of painting in particular, and that of moving the passions, are obtained most effectually by the use of licenses; which a rigid critic might censure as rendering the author's plan disproportioned, and his Composition incorrect. Thus we might pronounce with truth, that an orator, by working up the colours with studied attention in which some capital object is pourtrayed, and by endeavouring to catch *every* light in which it can be exposed to advantage, may give one branch of his subject greater compass and extent than it ought to possess. The same remark may be made of his address to the passions, in which the transitions may be too rapid, the appeals too daring, and the topics of expostulation may hang together with too much *seeming* negligence

---

into *foreign provinces*, are marked with such genuine strokes of nature and originality, as that the deviation from a rule is wholly absorbed in the contemplation of the effect.

to render the difcourfe ftrictly conformed to the rules of criticifm. But the ftandard of nature, and that of art, are effentially different in the cafes here examined. The firft would lead us to enquire whether the orator in one cafe has really placed the object of his attention in ftriking points of view; not whether thefe are numerous, but how far each is fignificant and interefting. In the other it would fuggeft to us, that we are not to try any *eloquent* performance by the tefts above enumerated, as decifive of its merit, but are to examine a much more important queftion for this purpofe, whether thefe correfpond to the natural feelings of a fufceptible temper. The avenues that lead to the heart of man are fo various as not to admit of regular enumeration. We cannot lay down general rules that are fufficiently comprehenfive of this fubject; but no man is at a lofs to decide on the tendency of a particular means to excite certain paffions or affections, becaufe of this he is rendered fenfible by feeling. Sudden tranfitions have a powerful effect upon many occafions, sions, when the heart is to be penetrated; because nothing is more natural in circumstances of real distress, than to fly to some prospect whose connection with that which engrosseth attention, may after all be merely ideal. Appeals in the same manner, and abjurations rendered energetical by certain awful and solemn circumstances, are the natural expressions of passion; and will be judged more or less excusable in particular cases, in proportion to the strength or imbecility of the mind before which they are presented. A man of weak feelings, and whose exertions are proportionably feeble, will be stunned, and, as it were, overpowered by an expression which one of vigorous intellects would have considered only as adequate to the occasion. Nature is likewise happily imitated by an apparently negligent disposition of objects, when the passions are to be stimulated, which hath, in this case, much greater efficacy than could have arisen from the closest and most exact arrangement. The mind, when giving vent to its sensations under the pressure of affliction, is attentive only

only to the strength of its expression, as conveying these with adequate emphasis. But as its ideas at that time succeed each other without much regularity, and are thrown into language as they occur, an imitation of this disorder, happily executed, is a picture of the human heart, and will be censured only by those who are either deprived of sensibility, or who have not attended to its effects.

Since, therefore, it will be said, these licenses have a noble effect in so many cases, at what point does this effect terminate, and in what instances are such liberties really inconsistent with correct Composition?—Principally in the three following.

1. When so little regard is paid to the established order of parts, as that one power of the mind breaks in abruptly upon the province of another, without aiding it in the accomplishment of its particular purpose. 2. When an author, not satisfied with attracting his reader's astonishment by superior excellence at one time, attempts to excite this passion too indiscriminately,

criminately, and thus aſſumes liberties upon every occaſion, which a great one can only juſtify. 3. When ſtrokes of perfect originality, whoſe connection with the principal ſubject is at beſt remote, are purſued through circumſtances ſo various and complicated as eraſe it wholly from our memory.

A judicious author will guard with particular ſolicitude againſt the two firſt mentioned indulgences, becauſe by breaking the union of parts in his piece, and by deſtroying its effect, theſe exhibit ſtriking evidences of defective underſtanding. An orator, who in the firſt part of his diſcourſe ſimply proves the truth of ſome propoſition, addreſſeth himſelf wholly to the reaſon of his hearers. Strokes, therefore, however admirable when contemplated apart, which are derived from another power, and are introduced without any tendency to promote his ultimate purpoſe, may be juſtly cenſured; not merely as uſeleſs ſuperfluities, but as foreign circumſtances thrown without order or propriety into a diſcourſe. Theſe, by leading
the

the mind away from the point of which it is in purfuit, inftead of throwing light upon it, tend to violate an effential law, and break that harmony with which the fubordinate parts of a fubject ought to concur in promoting a general end *.

Imagina-

---

* Among the ancient and illuftrious orators of Greece and Rome, there are few examples to be met with of the fault mentioned in the text. But this defect is amply fupplied by the rhetoricians of the middle and dark ages, as well as by modern writers of this clafe. It is difagreeable to felect examples of fuch a nature from works of real ingenuity. One however, we fhall adduce here for the fake of the *Englifh* reader, from a late collection of difcourfes which are diftinguifhed, upon the whole, by no inconfiderable fhare of eloquence. The ingenious Mr. Seed, in a difcourfe on the duty of unreferved obedience, propofeth to obviate this objection to his doctrine ;—that it is inconfiftent with the divine goodnefs to confign any man, who ftands clear of all other vices, to future mifery for one habitual fin. To this he replies, That future mifery is the neceffary confequence of one habit of fin, fince one habit of fin difqualifies us for the enjoyment of heaven.—That habitual bad difpofition, fays he, which the decays of the body do not weaken, the diffolution of it will not deftroy.—The joys of heaven (fays he) are like the beams of light: if they fall upon fome objects of a fuitable texture to reflect them, as upon cryftal, for inftance, they brighten and beautify them : but if upon others, they are quite loft

and

Imagination, it is true, may here be permitted to throw strong and lively colours on the objects that are succeffively contemplated. But in this office, it will be observed, that she acts only a secondary part, by setting off rational sentiments to the highest possible advantage, and thus impressing these upon the mind with a force which they must otherwise have wanted:

---

and stifled; they present nothing to the view, but one undistinguished blackness of darkness.—This metaphor, the reader will observe, hath no propriety as an illustration of the author's reply to the objection here proposed, but is so general and unappropriated, as to admit of an application to almost any religious rule. A correct writer will never indulge his imagination in a licence of this kind, even though it may have peculiar excellence when contemplated as a distinct picture, (which is not the case in the present instance), because it bears no relation to a point upon which every circumstance ought to throw light; and from which such as are foreign ought to be excluded, for the same reason, that when employed in any business that attracts very close attention, we abstract ourselves from such conversation as might draw off our thoughts from this point; or such external objects as might divert our eye. We consider not in this case, what attractions either of these may possess, had we been disengaged; but avoid them at the time only as having no relation to our employment.

wanted:—whereas in the cafe cenfured, this power intrudes as a principal when it ought to be wholly fubordinate; and inftead of promoting the fearch of truth, prefents objects wholly foreign to fuch a difquifition.

If a writer may thus be cenfured with juftice, who permits one power of the mind to interfere in the province of another, by throwing into it ftrokes that are foreign to the fubject, we may furely animadvert with the fame propriety upon Compofition, in which, by an attempt to excite admiration indifcriminately, every part appears to be over-wrought; and the liberties taken at all times are feldom juftified by the occafion. Even though this attempt had no tendency to render Compofition inaccurate, good fenfe would fuggeft to the mind, that it muft defeat the purpofe which it propofeth to bring about, even fuppofing it to be purfued with fuccefs; becaufe an object or idea that is truly admirable, in order to make an adequate impreffion, ought to be placed among fuch as have a fubordinate relation to it. By this means, the

the capital figure is difposed properly, fo, as to produce its full effect, and receives fome additional grace from each of thofe that furround it. Whereas, when we endeavour to fhow all objects in the *fame light*, and to excite promifcuoufly one uniform paffion, a work not only ceafeth to become interefting by being deprived of juft variety, but thoughts deftroy mutually the effect of each other; and the glare that is caft on all parts prevents us from fingling out, and from being duly impreffed by thofe which we might otherwife have dwelt on with admiration.

But it is principally to our prefent purpofe to obferve, that the licence is here carried too far; and Compofition is rendered fo incorrect by this practice, as to lie open to the jufteft cenfure. For as the judgment of that writer muft be defective in a very great degree, which cannot eftimate the comparative value of objects, fo as not to know that fome would be rendered ridiculous by being reprefented in colours that are fuited to others with propriety; fo the work of fuch a mind muft exhibit marks of this defect, so universal as to render the whole disgusting to a reader of penetration, when considered as a body that ought to have consistence and stability, in whatever manner he might be affected by the view of particular objects *.

The licence in the last place, of digressing from the principal point upon some occasions, which is claimed by all writers promiscuously as accomplishing purposes of importance, is then carried beyond its proper bound, when either repeated so frequently as to distract attention, or pursued through so many circumstances as to throw the subject which it was introduced to illustrate, wholly out of the reader's eye. A discourse, in which this conduct is pursued, can have no more connection than a dream made up of incoherent ideas, and must argue an indulgence of imagination

---

* The Thebais of Statius affords many examples of the fault here censured, as that writer appears to be particularly fond of dressing up every object in pompous and affected ornaments. This conduct often prevents the effect of his descriptions. The reader may apply, as an example of this kind, the passage quoted from him, sect. v.

wholly unwarrantable, as it is carried on in opposition to every rule that is established by reason*.

The observations we have made here, upon the abuse of the inventive faculty in the art of persuasion, bear so obvious a relation to that of poetry, as to require no particular application. The only circumstances by which the last mentioned art is peculiarly distinguished, are the freer use of high colouring in all subjects; and those irregular sallies of imagination which command admiration merely on account of their wildness and sublimity, and whose introduction would justly be deemed inexcusable in any other species of Composition. These are of two kinds: the first is constituted by the exhibition, though perhaps somewhat abrupt, of some bold

---

* As no poet, either ancient or modern, riseth to more astonishing grandeur than the *Theban Bard*, so from none do we meet with such instances of an incoherence wholly unwarrantable. The Ode inscribed Θρασιδαιω Θηβαιω Παιδι Σταδιει, ΠΥΘ. I. A. is wholly of this kind. The imagination of the poet, uncontrouled by any other power, renders this piece wholly excentric, and inexcusably obscure.

and masterly figure; or by an allegorical representation, pursued through various circumstances, as expressive of some great idea. The other arises from apostrophes strongly animated, from daring and original expressions thrown into a picture, which give *a grace* to the whole, that renders it truly and *properly admirable*. Of these we may observe, that not only are they confined to the pathetic art, but it is wholly into those branches of it which afford the widest range to the power of invention, that they can be dashed (if we may thus express it) without giving offence. The great master of the epopœa, has eminently distinguished his principal work by excellence of the former kind *;
and

---

* The philosophy of the Iliad, and the knowledge that Homer had acquired of nature, is conveyed in a series of allegories the most exquisitely beautiful that the human mind can be supposed to conceive. Every object appears to be animated with life, by the *creative touch* of this exalted genius; and hence ariseth that perpetual succession of inchanting forms, which keep attention always awake, while we are reading a work which must have otherwise excited unavoidable satiety from the uniformity of its subject. Among strokes
thus

and some modern performances of the highest

thus constantly diversified, there are some distinguished by their originality so strongly, as to fix the mind in admiration, and whose wild beauty more than contemplates for the defect of strict propriety. Let us take one example. It is in the description of Achilles, upon whose appearance Homer has lavished all the powers of his genius, when opposed in his last combat to Hector. After having placed successively before the eye his armour, his shield, the plumage of his helmet, his terrific aspect, eagle speed, and godlike demeanor, he paints him at last in the act of waving his spear, and considering in what place his adversary is vulnerable. On this occasion, the *very point of this hero's spear* must be irradiated while yet waving in the air, in order to complete the representation. Observe the illustration.

Οιος δ' αςηρ εισι μετ' αςρασι νυκτος αμολγω
Εσπερος, ος καλλιςος εν ουρανω ιςαται αςηρ·
Ως αιχμης απελαμπ' ευηκεος, ην αρ' Αχιλλευς
Παλλεν δεξιτερη.— ΙΛΙΑΔ. Χ.

In order to have rendered this illustration *strictly proper*, Achilles ought to have been placed among many warriors whose spears were all waving together, but his throwing a stronger light around him than any of the others. But who would lose this exquisitely beautiful and picturesque circumstance, for a small impropriety, which after all it is impossible to guard against in every instance, without giving up the noblest and most sublime exertions of human genius? In the same spirit he describes the eyes of Hector in another place, as withering all the strength of Greece. Nothing can exceed

highest poetic merit, afford the most striking examples of the latter *.

III. We exceed the *wild* beauty of the expression in which this idea is conveyed.

Εκτωρ δ' αμφιπεριστρωφα καλλιτριχας ιππους,
ΓΟΡΓΟΥΣ ΟΜΜΑΤ' ΕΧΩΝ.   ΙΛΙΑΔ. Θ.

This is undoubtedly " snatching a grace beyond the reach of art," if any thing can be it. Perhaps some readers will consider, as a more striking example of the licence which a great imagination may indulge without censure, the following sublime figure set before the mind in the highest colouring which that faculty can throw on any object. It is the description of the Origin of Time, in the Night Thoughts, a work inferior to none of the sentimental kind in point of *poetical* merit. Speaking of the abuse of time, the poet says,

Not on these terms was time (heaven's stranger) sent
On this important embassy to man.
When the DREAD SIRE on *emanation bent*,
And *big with nature* rising in his thought
Call'd forth creation!——
Not on these terms, from the great days of heav'n.
From *old eternity's mysterious orb*,
Was TIME *cut off*, and cast beneath the skies.

This we must, no doubt, acknowledge, has little connection with the sentiment immediately preceding, in which we are informed, that in no instance does this god (as he is called) stand neuter. The succeeding lines correspond still less to it. But is there a mind animated with the *least spark of sensibility*, which would dash out so great an effort of the most exalted genius, merely on this account?—Surely not. There is

some-

Observations on Composition.

III. We have now, in following out the method laid down in the beginning of this section,

---

something noble even in the irregularities of a great mind, in which the preservation of its *radical character* (when an *adequate subject* is presented to it), distinguisheth it from one of an inferior order, and converts its very defects into excellencies!—

* There is, perhaps, no writer, either ancient or modern, who has more the art of rendering his figures intensely animated and picturesque by certain daring and masterly strokes thrown out abruptly, than the divine author of Paradise Lost. His well known description of Death, opposed to Satan in his journey through Chaos, is wrought up with some which are truly original.

—— Black it stood as night,
Fierce as *ten furies*, terrible as hell, &c.
Again,
The monster moving onward came
With horrid strides;—*hell trembled as he strode*.

Admirable, however, as these are, the following strokes thrown into the description of Tasso's Pluto, is in no respect inferior to either.

Rossegian gli occhi, e di veneno infelto,
Come infausta cometa il guargo splende.

The portentuous glare of the comet flasheth suddenly upon the eye of the reader, and renders its original perfectly picturesque. It is one of those daring images which a great genius can only adopt, and which we contemplate, not with censure, but astonishment.— We should swell this note to too great length by adducing many examples of those expressions, distinguished

section, endeavoured to show what is understood by the term *correct*, when applied in its most extensive sense to Composition; what degree of attention a judicious writer will bestow on this character in the various departments of science; in what cases

---

guished by wildness or sublimity, which claim admiration in poetry. Let us, however, just mention one of the sudden apostrophe that so powerfully excites this passion. When Macbeth is just setting about the murder of Duncan, and has dismissed his servant, we expect from him some discourse, intermixed with expressions of horror and remorse, which the mind naturally suggests on the eve of some desperate and wicked attempt. But instead of these, his entranced imagination presents to him a dreadful object, and he breaks out at once into the exclamation,
 Is this a *dagger* that I see before me,
 The handle tow'rd my hand?—Come let me
  clutch thee!
and a little after,
  I see thee still,
 And on thy blade and dudgeon gouts of blood,
 Which was not so before.
This address is more abrupt and daring, than any of which a studied discourse could have admitted, in which the passions were to be excited by rules, however closely these might be adhered to. But *here* it strikes with irresistible energy, and is admirable as a deviation from those very laws, whose application in an inferior branch of the art, would have led us to censure any similar indulgence as a violation of order.

this

this attention may be carried too far; and, laftly, we have attempted to afcertain the bounds within which the licence of difpenfing with rules that is fometimes claimed by, and allowed to genius in fome inftances, ought always to be confined. It remains only, in order to render our view of this fubject complete, that we point out the moft proper methods of acquiring an excellence fo univerfally attended to; as neceffary to fum up our obfervations on the moft diftinguifhing characters of the art.

We fhall enter moft effectually into the queftion which it is here propofed to examine, by confidering Compofition in its moft extenfive latitude, as confifting of the union of fentiment and expreffion*. As no

---

* Quintilian ftates this point with great propriety. "Proxima ftylo Cogitatio eft, quæ & ipfa vires ab hoc accepit, & eft inter fcribendi laborem, extemporalemque fortunam, media quædam, & nefcio an ufus frequentiffimi."—Again he fays. " Neque vero rerum ordinem modo (quod ipfum fatis erat) intra fe, ipfa (cogitatio) difpofuit, fed verba etiam copulat, totamque ita contexit orationem, ut nihil ei præter manum debet."

no performance can be pronounced correct in which there is not a just correspondence betwixt these; and as we have already shown that they are not necessarily connected with each other, in the same manner as a cause and an effect; we shall examine separately by what methods each may appear in the least exceptionable light, and the concurrence of both may effectuate that purpose which it is proposed ultimately to obtain.

1. To render the sentiment of Composition correct, considered wholly as a distinct branch of the art, the following things appear to be necessary. 1. That the thoughts should have a strict relation to some principal point, and grow, 'as it were, naturally out of the subject. 2. That these, instead of being treated in the same uniform manner, should be explained with a care proportioned to their nature, and degrees of importance. 3. That they

---

debet." The reader of taste will be pleased with the last words of the sentence particularly, which express the author's meaning with much elegance. Instit. lib x. c. 6.

should be ranged in perspicuous order, so as gradually to open upon the mind of the reader, and place the ultimate end clearly and forcibly in his view, as he makes his approach to it.

1. By thoughts that grow out of a subject, we understand such as naturally tend to produce that effect, whether of proof, illustration, persuasion, or description, to which they are applied. When this tendency ceaseth to take place, *correct design* is essentially violated; nor is the department in which an author is employed of any consequence, as an apology for an indulgence of this kind. In order to obtain a point of such consequence, the writer ought not only to keep his eye steadily fixed both on the general end, and on the subordinate purposes which he may accomplish in the course of his procedure; but as it is difficult, especially in works of length, and when the parts are complicated; to avoid the intermixture of *foreign* objects with those that are directly to the purpose, he ought to revise his performance when his mind is cooled, at intervals

of leisure, from the ardor excited by a constant fluctuation of ideas*; and exclude from it those sentiments, however just or striking when viewed apart, which he discovers to be protuberances that disfigure his work; or such useless members of it as may be lopped off without injuring its proportion †. It will, no doubt, require considerable resolution to carry this admonition *steadily* into practice, because vanity (the most powerful of the passions) must be mortified by it; and the attractive or entertaining, give place to the useful. But this sacrifice will be made with less reluctance when it is considered, that by divesting Composition of such adventitious and frivolous circumstances, the effect of what is retained will be more sensibly felt, and every thought, as of importance to the

---

* " Hæc (Cogitatio) inter medios rerum actus, aliquid invenit vacui, nec otium patitur." Id. ibid.

† Εκ της αυχγως του επιχειρηματος ανισαμενου τε κεφαλαιου κατα το εφ' εξης υψος EN ο λογος γεννηται, και σωμα, μη διασπωμενος εν ταις υποφωραις, αλλα αυτος αυτε δοκων εχεσθαι, και .ανιςασθαι δι εαυτε. ΕΡΜΟΓΕΝ. περι Ευρησ. Σχημ. 12.

end

end in view, will make *that* impreſſion which ought moſt naturally to ariſe from it. Thoughts, on the contrary, or embelliſhments that tend rather to ſhow an author's genius, than to promote his purpoſe, while they gratify a temporary deſire, eſſentially injure his work. By diverting the mind to objects foreign from the point to be contemplated, theſe make it loſe that thread which would have led it by eaſy ſteps, if kept always in poſſeſſion, to the end originally propoſed.

2. As ſentiments, in order to be correct, ought in this manner to have a clear relation to ſome ultimate purpoſe, it is no leſs neceſſary that an author ſhould vary his method of unfolding or enforcing theſe, according to their natures and degrees of importance. No man needs to be informed, indeed, that ſome thoughts either as being more abſtracted in their nature, or demanding illuſtration from the place which theſe occupy, or, finally, in conſequence of the weight that reſts upon them in any branch of Compoſition, require to be explained with greater compaſs and

pre-

precifion than fuch as are recommended by none of thefe diftinctions. But ready as we are to make this general acknowledgment, it happens frequently, that the moft frivolous parts of a fubject are thofe upon which the greateft attention appears to have been beftowed; a conduct that naturally renders the whole obfcure, and deftroys its effect. This propenfity takes its rife often in men of genius, from the defire of obtaining a certain end as quickly as poffible; in the purfuit of which they go forward with fuch rapidity as prevents them from contemplating at leifure, the various means that conduce to its attainment. In confequence of this conduct, the author's inclination takes the lead at many times of his underftanding; and inftead of unfolding at length, and with particular accuracy thofe branches of a fubject, or thoughts which though perhaps the leaft fhowy, are yet of the greateft importance, he expatiates improperly on parts that are recommended by novelty, or may be laid open with the greateft facility. Impartial reflection muft fuggeft to us the many disadvantages arising from this indulgence of an unwarrantable propensity, by which a man, capable of thinking deeply as well as clearly, gives up his pretensions to both, in order to follow a whimsical bias; and deprives his performance of its principal merit by attempting to fix the reader's attention most intensely on those objects which contribute least to promote the scope he hath in view.

It is by an effort of judgment, not exerted at different times, but carried uniformly into exercise, that the consequences of indulging this bias will be prevented. The mind, it is no doubt true, may be misled in its estimation of objects, so as to permit the frivolous to take place of the useful in the heat of Composition; in the same manner as a man of discernment in characters, may prefer tinselled ostentation to merit modestly attired, while he is hurried by business, or duped by prejudice:— but in both cases, it is by recollection that the error is detected; and the trivial displaced, however elaborately decorated, to make

make way for what has real utility *. By
neglecting to purfue a courfe fuch as is
here

---

* The obfervations made on this fubject may require perhaps to be exemplified, as many readers, who are not accuftomed to fearch out the lefs obvious excellencies of Compofition, and who want leifure for this tafk, may be at a lofs to apply general remarks on fuch a theme, until they are thrown into the proper track. It happens luckily for us at prefent, that in a periodical performance of diftinguifhed merit, we meet with an example perfectly to the purpofe. Addifon fays, in one of his Spectators, that "notwithftanding " we fall fhort at prefent of the ancients, in poetry, " painting, oratory, hiftory, architecture, and all the " noble arts and fciences, which depend more upon " genius than experience; we *exceed them* as much " in doggerel, humour, burlefque, and all the trivial " arts of ridicule."—This fine obfervation (it is well remarked by the author of that excellent paper, entitled, the Adventurer), ftands in the form of a *general affertion*. He examines, therefore, its truth by an induction of particulars, and confirms it by examples: Adven. vol. iv. No. 127, 133. Without entering particularly into the truth of this remark (as to which we might differ from both thefe writers, refpectable as they are), we may only obferve from it, that thoughts that are of much ufe when enforced with a certain degree of energy, may yet be overlooked by the greater number of readers, when the *proper emphafis*, if we may thus exprefs it, is not laid upon them by the writer; and though it is otherwife in the cafe here fpecified, yet neither hath an author reafon to
expect

here pointed out, works in which there is a very high degree of merit are rendered obscure to the greater number of readers; nor can their opinion be censured as rash or ill-founded. For however intrinsically excellent many sentiments may be in a work of which these ought to constitute the principal ornaments, yet it is not surely the reader's business to search them out, if they are placed in disadvantageous points of light by the writer. The latter may direct the attention of the former to run in any channel that he may cut out for it. If parts, therefore, com-

---

expect that his readers in general will be qualified to feel the force of truths, even the most important, when not confirmed by satisfactory evidence; nor if they should, that any of them, like the present ingenious critic, not satisfied with his own perception of such a truth, will endeavour likewise to render its influence and evidence universal. He, therefore, who fixeth his attention upon the point of utility, ought always to remember, that in order to gain this end, he must seldom *assert* without entering into the proof of his principles; and that it will often be necessary for him to act in opposition to the impulse of inclination, when reason informs him that by complying with it, he will at least conceal what has genuine excellence; if he does not really sacrifice it altogether to objects that are comparatively frivolous and useless.

paratively

paratively mean are wrought up so highly as to conceal those that are of greater consequence, he is under obligation to the few who may clear these diamonds from the rubbish that surrounds them, but ought to consider, as the effect of so injudicious a conduct, the censure which will in general be past upon the whole, as either unintelligible, or containing little to the purpose.

That the error here exposed may be effectually avoided, a judicious writer will find it necessary to guard against the impulse of imagination, as this power, even when it subsists in the highest degree, is always ready to bestow the highest colouring on thoughts that strike by their brilliance, rather than on sentiments that impress conviction by their importance. This is a point which it rather demands resolution, than any great degree of attention to carry into practice. A moderate share of this last will enable an author to distinguish objects of real utility, from such as are adventitious, or ornamental. But it may require no inconsiderable effort to cancel a favourite illustration, not because

cause inadequate to its pattern, but merely
as an unneceffary embellifhment; and to
fubftitute in its place, the proof of fome
propofition that may have been defectively
laid open; the completion of fome evidence that may not have been fuitably
enforced; or the illuftration of a thought
lefs fufceptible of ornament; and to render
which energetical, fancy is brought with
difficulty to give her concurrence. *Habit*,
therefore, is every thing in fuch cafes as
the prefent. When the mind hath been
accuftomed to examine its productions,
with the view of placing in ftrong lights
fuch objects as have primary confequence,
without regarding them merely as agreeable; reafon will acquire by degrees fo
much command over the other powers,
that even when ideas are crouding together moft clofely, and when imagination
catcheth fome with eagernefs, it will check
the career of this faculty; and will render
its images fubfervient to the purpofe of elu-
cidating points of importance, fo as to prevent future and difagreeable emendations.

3. We mentioned, as the laft circumftance neceffary to render the fentiment of

any performance correct, its being placed in such exact disposition as gradually to open with new evidence upon the mind of the reader as he proceeds, that the ultimate purpose of the work may be shown in a clear and striking light as we approach to it. To go about to prove that thoughts cannot be correctly or judiciously put together, when this regularity is not observed, would be wholly impertinent. We have enlarged at so much length on the subject of method in every branch of Composition, that without falling into repetition, little can be added on this point. In order to be thoroughly master of a subject (especially of one that is comprehensive) an author ought to weigh the principal topics separately in his mind, and to turn each upon every side, so as to judge of the lights in which it may be exposed to the best advantage. After having marked down such observations as occur to him on each part contemplated by itself, it will be proper for him to compare them together; that he may judge of their mutual coherence, as well as of their extent, as including what is necessary to be advanced.

vanced *. When the writer hath once formed a general eftimate of this kind, with whofe accuracy he is fatisfied, he hath only further to take care in the delineation of particular parts, that his eye when taking cognifance of one object, may not be diverted to others, as being fimilar, until his firft purpofe is accomplifhed; becaufe the mind is unavoidably embarraffed by having things of different kinds prefented before it at the fame time, and can delineate neither with precifion. On the other hand, when never lofing fight of his principal end, an author proceeds through the intermediate fteps with deliberate recollection †, he will moft probably accomplifh his own defign effectually, by taking in every means that conduceth to gain it;

---

* This procedure conftitutes what an ancient critic denominates ΤΟ ΠΡΕΠΟΝ ΤΗΣ ΤΑΞΙΩΣ, the Decency of Order, which he afcribes fo particularly to Lyfias. Ληπτεον δε το πρεπον της ταξιως παρα Λυσιν. ΔΙΟΝΥΣ. ΛΥΣ.

† To this purpofe is the judicious Roman's obfervation.

Ordinis hæc virtus erit & venus eft, aut ego fallor
Ut jam nunc dicet, jam nunc debentia dici
Pleraque differat, & prefens in tempus omittat. Hor.

and

and will place each of these in its proper place so distinctly before his readers, as at the same time to impress conviction upon his understanding, and the knowledge of the means that produced it upon his memory.

2. Thus far we have endeavoured to show what requisitions are necessary to render sentiment, considered by itself, as the most important branch of Composition, properly correct. In order to obtain this character in perfection, it is, however, indispensibly necessary, that a just correspondence of language to thoughts thus accurately disposed should take place *, as without this harmonious concurrence the composition must be essentially defective.
—This

---

* Της μεντοι αγωγης των περιοδων το κυκλικν. Και των σχηματισμων της λεξεως το μειρακιωδες ουκ εδοκιμαζον. Δουλευει γαρ η Διανοια, πολλακις τω ρυθμω της λεξεως, και τω κομψω λειπεται το αληθινον. Βυλεται δε η Φυσις τοις νοημασιν επεισθαι την λεξιν, *	 τη λεξει τα νοηματα. ΔΙΟΝΥΣ. ΑΛΙΚΑΡ. ΙΣΩΚ. It may not be improper to subjoin this critic's judgment with regard to the most perfect expression, from his excellent treatise Περι ΣΥΝΘΕΣ. ΟΝΩΜ. Εστι λεξις ΚΡΑΤΙΣΤΗ ΠΑΣΩΝ, η τις αν εχοι πλειςας αναπαυλας και μεταβολας αρμονιας, οταν τοτε μεν εν περιοδω λεγηται, τοτε δε ΕΞΩ περιοδου. Και η δε μεν η περι-

This last is (as we have already shown) a consequence invariably arising from the former. Obscurity in the manner of expressing ideas, indicates always some embarrassment in their original formation; and he who is able to separate these, and range them under proper heads, will never be at a loss (if he bestows suitable attention on this circumstance) to convey them to the minds of others with adequate perspicuity. As we have endeavoured in canvassing this branch of our subject, to shew in what manner every character of the style of Composition may be obtained in the highest perfection, we refer the reader to the concluding article of each preceding section, for satisfaction on this head, along with what is said on it in the present.

η περιοδος εκ πλειονων πλεκηται κολων ; ηδε δε εξ ελαττονων. Αυτων δε των κολων το μεν βραχυτερον το δε μακροτερον, &c. Vid. Rapin. ΔΙΟΝΥΣ. ΣΥΓΓΡΑΜ, tom. ii. p. 29. edit. Lip.

FINIS.

www.ingramcontent.com/pod-product-compliance
Lightning Source LLC
Chambersburg PA
CBHW020233240426
43672CB00006B/513